The Claude Finance Playbook

Structured Mega-Prompts for Investment Banking, Valuation, and Deal Strategy

The Claude Finance Playbook

Structured Prompts for Investment Banking, Valuation, and Deal Strategy

Stelvin Saji

Author's Note

Finance has long been a discipline defined by structure, rigor, and precision. From valuation models to complex deal negotiations, the language of investment banking and corporate strategy has always relied on clarity of thought and disciplined frameworks. With the emergence of advanced artificial intelligence systems such as Claude, a new frontier has opened, one where human expertise and machine intelligence can work together to elevate financial analysis to unprecedented levels.

The Claude Finance Playbook was written with a single objective: to help professionals harness AI not as a shortcut, but as a strategic thinking partner. In modern finance, the difference between ordinary analysis and exceptional insight often lies in how questions are framed. Structured prompting allows analysts, bankers, consultants, and founders to transform AI from a generic assistant into a precise analytical tool capable of supporting valuation, financial modeling, due diligence, and deal strategy.

This book is not about replacing financial judgment. On the contrary, it is about strengthening it. AI performs best when guided by disciplined thinking, the same thinking that defines elite professionals in investment banking, private equity, venture capital, and corporate finance. By structuring prompts correctly, we can extract deeper insights, challenge assumptions, and accelerate analytical workflows while maintaining the intellectual rigor that the financial world demands.

Throughout these pages, you will find frameworks designed to mirror the real processes used in high-level finance: breaking down valuation assumptions, evaluating strategic transactions, analyzing risks, and structuring deal narratives. Each prompt is crafted to encourage clarity, precision, and strategic thinking. My hope is that this playbook becomes more than a technical guide. I hope it becomes a toolkit for professionals who want to think sharper, analyze deeper, and operate at a higher level in an increasingly AI-augmented world. Finance has always evolved alongside technology, from spreadsheets to algorithmic trading. Structured prompting represents the next stage of that evolution. Those who learn to use it effectively will not only work faster; they will think better.

Contents

Framework 4: Solo Sales Engine & Revenue Conversion Framework

Framework 5: Solo Business Scaling & Leverage Optimization Framework

Papers

Introduction

Artificial intelligence is rapidly transforming how professionals analyze information, generate insights, and make decisions. In fields like finance, where structured reasoning, data interpretation, and strategic thinking are essential, AI has the potential to become an incredibly powerful analytical partner. Yet despite this potential, most professionals are not using AI systems effectively.

Across online communities and platforms, thousands of prompts circulate every day claiming to unlock sophisticated financial analysis. Many of them promise to transform an AI model into an "investment banker," a "financial analyst," or a "strategy consultant". But the reality is that most of these prompts are surprisingly simple.

A typical prompt might say something like:

"Act as an investment banker and analyze this company."

At first glance, this appears reasonable. After all, the instruction clearly defines a role. But when examined more closely, it lacks the essential elements that make real financial analysis meaningful.

There is no analytical framework.
There are no methodological constraints.
There is no structured output format.

In other words, the prompt does not guide the AI through the disciplined reasoning processes that professionals in finance rely on every day. This gap, between simple prompting and structured analytical thinking is the central problem this book aims to address.

The Importance of Structure

Financial analysis is not simply a collection of opinions or observations. It is a structured discipline built on frameworks that guide how analysts evaluate businesses, industries, and strategic opportunities. Investment bankers, equity researchers, and financial strategists rarely approach problems with vague instructions. Instead, they rely on established methodologies such as valuation models, competitive analysis frameworks, and structured risk evaluation. These frameworks serve an important purpose: they create consistency, clarity, and rigor in the analytical process. Without structure, financial analysis quickly becomes speculative. With structure, it becomes systematic and defensible.

Artificial intelligence operates in a similar way. When prompts are vague, the responses tend to be generic. But when prompts introduce structured methodologies, constraints, and clearly defined outputs, AI models begin to produce results that are far more thoughtful and sophisticated.

This is particularly true for modern AI systems such as Claude, which have demonstrated strong capabilities in reasoning-intensive tasks. Benchmarks conducted by organizations like Wall Street Prep suggest that Claude performs well in structured financial scenarios, sometimes outperforming other widely used AI tools such as GitHub Copilot and ChatGPT when the prompts are carefully designed. However, these results are not automatic. They depend heavily on how the interaction with the AI is structured.

From Simple Prompts to Structured Mega-Prompts

The difference between a weak AI output and a powerful one often comes down to the quality of the prompt. Simple prompts rely primarily on role assignments:

"Act as a financial analyst."
"Act as an investment banker."
"Act as a venture capitalist."

While these instructions provide context, they do not provide a method. Professional analysis requires something more deliberate. It requires prompts that defines:

- The analytical role
- The reasoning methodology
- The constraints applied to the analysis
- The structure of the output

When these components are combined effectively, the prompt becomes more than a simple instruction. It becomes a structured analytical framework that guides the AI through a disciplined reasoning process.

In this book, these frameworks are referred to as mega-prompts. A mega-prompt is not merely longer or more complex than a typical prompt. Instead, it is designed to mirror the intellectual structure of professional analytical workflows. Each mega-prompt acts as a blueprint for a specific type of financial reasoning, whether it involves evaluating a company's competitive position, analyzing financial statements, assessing potential acquisitions, or generating an investment thesis.

This book introduces eight structured mega-prompts designed specifically for financial analysis. Each prompt is built around analytical frameworks commonly used in areas such as:

- Investment banking
- Equity research
- Market intelligence
- Strategic evaluation
- Risk analysis

Rather than presenting prompts as isolated tricks, the book focuses on the underlying principles that make them effective. Readers will learn how to design prompts that guide AI models through disciplined reasoning processes and produce consistent analytical outputs. The goal is not to replace human expertise in finance. Instead, it is to augment that expertise by using AI as a structured analytical tool, one capable of exploring ideas, organizing information, and generating insights within well-defined frameworks.

When used thoughtfully, AI can help accelerate many aspects of the analytical process, from initial research to structured evaluation. But achieving this requires moving beyond simplistic prompting. It requires a more deliberate approach.

The Ultimate Claude Prompt Blueprint

Most users interact with Claude as if they're sending a casual message, an approach that works well for simple, one-off questions. However, when the goal is to elicit expert-level performance, a more structured method is required. To unlock Claude's full capabilities, it must be engaged with the clarity and precision of a system, not a conversation. XML tagging provides that structure. By organizing instructions into clearly defined components, it enables more accurate interpretation, better context handling, and consistently higher-quality outputs. This template introduces the underlying framework, explains the purpose of each tag, and equips you with a practical, ready-to-use system for advanced prompting.

Q. Why XML Tags Change Everything?

Claude is designed to recognize XML tags as clear structural boundaries. When instructions are organized within tags such as <role> or <task>, the model does more than simply read the content, it systematically parses it. This allows Claude to distinguish where a role definition ends and where a task begins, to separate contextual information from actionable instructions, and to interpret each component with greater precision.

The distinction is significant. A plain-text prompt presents all information as a single, unstructured stream, relying on the model to infer what is most important. In contrast, an XML-structured prompt explicitly defines each element and its purpose, guiding Claude on how to interpret and apply the information. The result is a more controlled, reliable, and high-quality output. The XML structure provides clear separation of context, enabling more precise and structured responses. It allows the model to distinguish between the assigned role, the task requirements, the business idea as input data, and the expected response format as the output specification. This compartmentalization improves clarity, focus, and overall quality of the analysis.

A normal plain text prompt:

```
I would like you to assume the role of a business strategist
and evaluate my startup concept. The idea is to develop a
mobile application designed specifically for dog walkers.

Please provide a comprehensive analysis that includes:

1. Key market risks and potential challenges
2. Target customer personas and their behaviors
3. Strategic recommendations on viability, differentiation, and
growth opportunities

I'm looking for a detailed, candid assessment that highlights
both strengths and weaknesses of the idea.
```

The same prompt but following the XML Structure:

```
<role> You are a pragmatic business strategist with expertise
in evaluating business ideas for real-world viability.
</role>

<task> Analyze the following business idea objectively. Assess
both its strengths and weaknesses, considering practical
execution challenges. Provide a candid, balanced evaluation
along with a clear recommendation.
</task>

<business_idea>
A mobile application that connects dog owners with vetted local
dog walkers, featuring real-time GPS tracking and automated
scheduling.
</business_idea>

<response_format>
Business overview, Three target customer personas with their
key pain points, Market risks and challenges, Alternative
business models or strategic variations & Final recommendation
</response_format>
```

The 8 Tags That Make a Mega-Prompt

You do not need to include every element in every prompt. Select only the components that are relevant to the specific task at hand. Think of this as a flexible framework rather than a mandatory checklist.

1. <role> - Defines the Model's Perspective

Use this section to specify the expertise or perspective the model should adopt. The more precise and context-rich the role definition, the more specialized and relevant the output will be.

- **Less effective:** You are a marketing expert.
- **More effective:** You are a conversion-focused email copywriter specializing in SaaS onboarding sequences for B2B products.

A well-defined role should clearly communicate three elements:

- The domain of expertise
- The specific area of specialization
- The relevant context (such as industry, audience, or application)

```
<role>
You are a conversion-focused email copywriter specializing
in B2B SaaS onboarding sequences. You prioritize clarity
over cleverness and consistently tie messaging to the
user's core pain points and desired outcomes.
</role>
```

2. <goal> - Definition of Success

This defines the overarching outcome you want to achieve, not the process or structure, but the end result. Limit this to 1–2 sentences. If it requires more, you're likely combining multiple objectives and should separate them into distinct prompts.

```
<goal>
Develop a 5-email onboarding sequence designed to
reduce churn within the first 14 days by directly
addressing the top three reasons users disengage
from the product.
</goal>
```

3. <key_tasks> - Execution Framework

Break the work into clearly numbered steps to ensure nothing is missed or executed out of order. Each step should represent a single, specific action.

```
<key_tasks>
Step 1: Determine the top three drivers of churn based on the provided user
feedback.
Step 2: Align each churn driver with a corresponding email in the sequence.
Step 3: Develop subject lines and body copy for all five emails.
Step 4: Define a recommended send schedule, including timing and rationale.
</key_tasks>
```

Q. When to omit this tag?

If the task can be fully expressed in a single, concise sentence, the <goal> tag alone is sufficient.

4. <response_structure> - Guidance for Response Style

This defines the tone, level of depth, and perspective of the response. It shapes how the output should be delivered, not how it's structured (that's handled by <response_format>).

```
<response_structure>
1. Deliver in-depth, practical guidance—avoid high-level or generic advice.
2. Maintain a clear, conversational tone without relying on corporate jargon.
3. Write from the perspective of a senior copywriter providing feedback on a junior's work.
4. Incorporate relevant SaaS examples to ground recommendations in real-world context.
</response_structure>
```

5. <session_structure> - Conversation Flow Guidelines

Use this structure when you want Claude to lead a multi-turn, guided interaction instead of providing a single comprehensive response. It defincs the expected flow and engagement pattern.

```
<session_structure>
1. Approach: Guided, step-by-step problem solving.
2. Begin by asking three clarifying questions about my product and target audience.
3. Once I respond, provide a draft outline of the sequence for my review and approval.
4. Proceed to write the full email sequence only after the outline has been approved.
</session_structure>
```

Q. When to omit this tag?

Exclude this section if you prefer a complete response in a single interaction.

6. <examples> - Demonstrating Expected Output Quality

Use this section to demonstrate what strong responses look like. Well-crafted examples are one of the most effective ways to guide Claude's output, often more impactful than detailed instructions alone. Include both the input and the desired output, and label them clearly for clarity and consistency.

```
<examples>
Example 1:
Input: "Users say the dashboard is confusing."
Output:
  Subject: Your dashboard, simplified
  Body: Hey [Name], we heard you. The dashboard can feel like a lot
  on day one. Here's a 2-minute video walkthrough that covers the
  3 panels you'll actually use daily...

Example 2:
Input: "Users forget to complete setup."
Output:
  Subject: You're 80% there (one step left)
  Body: Hey [Name], you started something good. Your account is set up,
  your team is invited, but there's one setting that unlocks [key feature]...
</examples>
```

7. <information_about_me> - Contextual Input for Personalization

Use this section to provide relevant details about your business, audience, product, or specific situation. This context serves as the foundation for Claude's responses. Include only information that directly supports your objective. Irrelevant details may reduce clarity and effectiveness.

```
<information_about_me>
1. Offering: TaskFlow, a SaaS platform built to help remote teams (10-50
members) manage projects efficiently
- Key reasons users leave:
  1) Interface feels overwhelming at first glance
  2) Users don't fully complete onboarding
  3) Missing integrations with tools they already rely on
2. Communication style: Conversational, clear, and approachable with a
lightly informal tone; avoid sounding overly corporate
3. Onboarding status: Currently limited to a single welcome email, with no
ongoing nurture or guidance sequence
</information_about_me>
```

8. <response_format> - Defining the Structure of the Output

Use this section to clearly specify the format and structure of the final response. Focus on how the output should be organized, rather than the tone or style of writing. Outline the exact components, order, and any constraints (such as length or layout) so the response is consistent and easy to use.

```
<response_format>
For every email, include the following elements:
1. Email sequence number along with the scheduled send timing (e.g.,
"Email 1 - Day 0")
2. A clear and compelling subject line
3. Body content ranging between 150-200 words
4. Call-to-action (CTA) button text
5. A brief internal note outlining the strategic intent behind the email

Present the output as a numbered list, not in table format.
</response_format>
```

Q. When to use each of these tags?

Tags	Use when you..	Skip when...
<role>	You need specialized expertise	Task is general knowledge
<goal>	**Always use this one!**	**Never skip it!**
<key_tasks>	Multi-step work with a specific order	Simple & Single Action Tasks
<response_ structure>	You care about tone, depth or persona	Default tone of Claude works fine on this
<session_ structure>	You want a multi-tone guided flow	Everything's in one shot
<examples>	Have a specific output style in mind	Exploring & want Claude's take on it
<information_ about_me>	Claude needs your specific context	Task is hypothetical/ generic
<response_ format>	Needs a specific output shape	Fine with Claude's default choosing

Comprehensive Prompt Template (Customizable Framework)

Use the structure below as a foundation for crafting clear, high-quality prompts. Adapt, rename, or remove sections as needed, what matters is the clarity of structure, not the exact tag names. You may tailor labels (e.g., <brand_info> instead of <information_about_me>, or <process_steps> instead of <key_tasks>) to suit your specific use case.

```
<role>
[Define the expert role to be assumed. Include domain expertise,
specialization, and relevant industry context.]
</role>

<goal>
[State the primary objective clearly in 1-2 concise sentences.]
</goal>

<key_tasks>
Step 1: [Describe the first action or responsibility]
Step 2: [Describe the second action or responsibility]
Step 3: [Describe the third action or responsibility]
</key_tasks>

<response_structure>
1. [Specify tone, depth, and level of detail]
2. [Indicate persona, perspective, or voice to adopt]
3. [Include any stylistic or formatting preferences]
</response_structure>

<session_structure>
1. [Define interaction style: single response or multi-turn dialogue]
2. [Clarify who leads the interaction: user or assistant]
3. [Outline checkpoints, validations, or approval stages if required]
</session_structure>

<examples>
Example 1:
Input: [Provide a representative input]
Output: [Provide the exact desired output]
</examples>

<information_about_me>
1. [Relevant detail #1]
2. [Relevant detail #2]
3. [Relevant detail #3]
</information_about_me>

<response_format>
[Define the exact output format: bullet list, table, narrative, code block, etc.]
[Include any constraints related to length, structure, or formatting]
</response_format>
```

To access a collection of ready-to-use prompts, please refer to page 191 and scan the QR code. From there, you can copy this template and begin customizing it to suit your needs.

Example Test Prompt

```
<role> You are a pragmatic business strategist with deep expertise in evaluating
business concepts for real world viability, scalability, and market fit.
</role>

<task> Conduct an objective and critical analysis of the business idea provided. Assess
both its strengths and potential weaknesses in a realistic market context. Develop
three distinct, theoretically grounded customer personas and present their candid
feedback. Conclude with a clear, direct validation and recommendation.
</task>

<business_idea>
A mobile application that connects dog owners with vetted local dog walkers, offering
features such as real-time GPS tracking and automated scheduling.
</business_idea>

<response_format>
Structure your response as follows:

1. Business idea overview (2-3 concise sentences)
2. Potential target markets
3. Three customer personas, each including: age, occupation, key pain points, and an
honest first-person reaction to the product
4. Key market risks and challenges
5. Alternative business models worth exploring

Final validation and recommendation (be direct and candid, avoid diplomatic language)
</response_format>
```

NOTE

The <response_format> tag outlines the desired structure using a numbered list, but it does not enforce a strict XML-style output. The intent is to guide the model's response organization while still allowing it to write naturally and fluidly. In other words, you are structuring the input expectations, not constraining the output into a rigid format, enabling more coherent and human-like responses within the defined framework.

Framework 1

The Discounted Cash Flow (DCF) Valuation Engine

In professional finance, the Discounted Cash Flow (DCF) valuation is considered one of the most rigorous and intellectually disciplined methods for determining the intrinsic value of a company. Investment bankers, equity research analysts, and corporate finance professionals rely on DCF analysis because it focuses on the fundamental drivers of a business, its ability to generate future cash flows and the risk associated with those cash flows. Unlike quick valuation shortcuts based solely on market multiples, a well-constructed DCF forces analysts to carefully examine revenue drivers, operating efficiency, capital expenditures, working capital dynamics, and long-term growth expectations. This process not only produces a valuation estimate but also reveals the underlying assumptions that shape the investment thesis.

However, building a credible DCF model is rarely a simple exercise. It requires a structured methodology, clear documentation of assumptions, and the discipline to stress-test results under different scenarios. In professional settings, analysts are expected to justify every input, from revenue growth forecasts to the cost of capital, while ensuring the final valuation aligns with market realities. The framework below is designed to replicate the analytical workflow used by senior investment banking analysts when performing a full DCF valuation. Instead of generating a single point estimate, the prompt emphasizes transparency, conservative assumptions, and sensitivity analysis so that the final output reflects a defensible valuation range supported by clearly articulated reasoning. By using this prompt, analysts, students, and finance professionals can systematically construct a complete DCF valuation with organized steps and structured outputs. The prompt guides the user through projecting free cash flows, calculating the weighted average cost of capital, estimating terminal value using multiple methods, and performing sensitivity analysis to understand how key assumptions influence the valuation range. With accurate financial data, this framework enables institution-grade valuation analysis used in professional finance.

DCF VALUATION MODEL

Role: Senior investment banking analyst specializing in DCF modeling for [INDUSTRY] companies.

Task: Build a complete discounted cash flow valuation for [COMPANY NAME].

Context: [Paste: 3 years of revenue, EBIT, capex, D&A, working capital changes, effective tax rate. Include current share price, shares outstanding, and net debt.]

Steps:

1. Project free cash flows for 5 years using bottom-up revenue drivers
2. Calculate WACC: use CAPM for cost of equity, flag your beta source
3. Apply terminal value using both Gordon Growth and exit multiple methods
4. Derive enterprise value and equity value per share
5. Build a sensitivity table: WACC (±100bps) vs terminal growth rate (±0.5%)

Goal: A defensible valuation with documented assumptions, not a point estimate.

Constraints: Flag every assumption lacking source data. Use conservative bias on growth rates. Reconcile DCF output against trading comps before concluding.

Output: Organized sections per step. Sensitivity table in plain text matrix format. Flag the 3 assumptions that most impact the valuation range.

Q. How Users Can Apply This Prompt?

Users can apply this prompt by first providing the relevant financial and market inputs for the company they wish to analyze. This includes three years of historical financial data, such as revenue, EBIT, capital expenditures, depreciation and amortization, working capital changes, and the effective tax rate, along with current market information like share price, shares outstanding, and net debt. Once this information is inserted into the context section, the prompt systematically instructs the model to construct a full DCF valuation. It begins by projecting five years of free cash flows using bottom-up revenue drivers, ensuring the forecast is grounded in operational logic rather than arbitrary growth assumptions. The framework then calculates the Weighted Average Cost of Capital (WACC) using the Capital Asset Pricing Model (CAPM) for the cost of equity, with explicit attention given to the source and credibility of the beta input.

Q. What the Prompt Produces?

After projecting cash flows and calculating the appropriate discount rate, the prompt guides the valuation toward estimating terminal value using two complementary approaches: the Gordon Growth (perpetual growth) method and an exit multiple method commonly used in investment banking analyses. These methods help establish a range for the company's long-term value. The analysis then derives the enterprise value, converts it into equity value, and calculates the implied value per share. Importantly, the framework also requires the construction of a sensitivity analysis that tests how changes in key assumptions, specifically WACC and terminal growth rate, affect the valuation outcome. By presenting this sensitivity in a clear matrix format, the prompt highlights how valuation can shift under different capital cost and growth scenarios.

Beyond simply calculating numbers, the prompt enforces the type of analytical discipline expected in professional finance environments. It requires the model to flag any assumptions that lack supporting data, apply conservative bias when projecting growth, and reconcile the DCF output against trading comparables before forming a conclusion. This ensures the valuation is not treated as a precise prediction but rather as a well-reasoned range supported by transparent assumptions. The final output also identifies the three assumptions that most significantly influence the valuation range, helping users understand where the model is most sensitive.

As a result, the prompt becomes more than a technical tool, it serves as a structured framework for producing defensible, institution-quality valuations that mirror the analytical standards used in investment banking, equity research, and corporate finance.

Framework 2
The Market Comps Valuation Model

In equity research and investment banking, Comparable Company Analysis (Comps) is one of the most widely used valuation methods for understanding how the market currently prices similar businesses. While intrinsic valuation models such as Discounted Cash Flow focus on the fundamental ability of a company to generate future cash flows, trading comps provide a market-based perspective by examining how investors value comparable companies operating in the same industry. By analyzing valuation multiples such as EV/Revenue, EV/EBITDA, EV/EBIT, and Price-to-Earnings, analysts can establish a realistic valuation range grounded in actual market behavior. This method is frequently used in deal advisory, equity research reports, and investment committee discussions because it reflects real-time investor sentiment and industry benchmarks.

COMPARABLE COMPANY ANALYSIS

Role: Equity research analyst at a top-10 investment bank specializing in [INDUSTRY] sector coverage.

Task: Build a trading comps analysis for [COMPANY NAME] to determine implied valuation ranges.

Context: [Paste: LTM revenue, EBITDA, EBIT, net income, net debt, shares outstanding, current market cap. Include 3-5 known competitor names if available.]

Steps:

1. Identify 10-12 publicly traded peers by business model similarity, revenue scale (0.5x–2x target), and geography
2. List standard trading multiples for each peer: EV/Revenue, EV/EBITDA, EV/EBIT, P/E (LTM and NTM)
3. Calculate mean, median, 25th, and 75th percentile for each multiple
4. Apply median range to the target to derive implied EV and share price
5. Flag peers that distort the median (outliers, M&A premiums)

Goal: A peer-reviewed valuation range presentable to a deal committee.

Constraints: Flag any peer where data is estimated rather than reported. Note sector-specific multiples that take precedence (e.g., Price/Book for banks, EV/EBITDAX for energy).

Output: Peer table in text format, multiple ranges, implied valuation summary, 2–3 sentence commentary on where the target should trade and why.

Q. How Users Can Apply This Prompt?

Users can apply this framework by first providing the necessary financial data for the target company, including LTM revenue, EBITDA, EBIT, net income, net debt, shares outstanding, and current market capitalization. If known competitors are available, they can also be included to help guide the peer selection process.

Once the context is provided, the prompt systematically constructs a trading comparables table, identifying a set of publicly traded peers with similar business characteristics and revenue scale. It then calculates key valuation multiples for each company and determines the statistical distribution across the peer group. Using the median and percentile ranges of these multiples, the analysis derives an implied enterprise value and share price range for the target company.

Beyond simply generating numbers, the prompt also highlights analytical discipline by flagging peers with estimated data, identifying outliers that distort the median, and acknowledging sector-specific valuation metrics when applicable. The final output presents a clear peer table, multiple ranges, and an implied valuation summary accompanied by concise commentary explaining where the target company should reasonably trade within the peer set. When used with reliable financial inputs, this framework enables users to produce a professional, deal-ready trading comps analysis similar to the standards used in institutional equity research and investment banking.

Framework 3

The Leveraged Buyout Modeling (LBO) Framework

In private equity investing, the Leveraged Buyout (LBO) model is one of the most critical tools used to evaluate whether a potential acquisition can generate attractive investor returns. Unlike other valuation methods that primarily estimate a company's intrinsic or market value, an LBO model focuses on how a transaction is financed and how leverage can amplify equity returns over time. Private equity firms rely on these models to analyze capital structures, project operational performance, and determine whether a deal can realistically meet the fund's target return thresholds. Because leveraged transactions involve significant financial risk and complex financing structures, the analysis must be structured, transparent, and grounded in realistic operating assumptions.

Constructing a reliable LBO model requires a disciplined approach that mirrors the workflow used by private equity associates and deal teams during the investment evaluation process. Analysts must carefully structure the transaction's sources and uses of capital, build a debt repayment schedule, forecast operational performance, and estimate the value of the business at exit.

This prompt is designed to replicate that professional modeling framework by guiding the user step by step through the key components of a leveraged buyout analysis. Rather than producing a simple return estimate, the framework emphasizes realistic leverage assumptions, consistent interest rate modeling, and scenario analysis across different exit multiples. By doing so, it allows the user to evaluate whether the transaction can generate the target internal rate of return (IRR) typically required by private equity funds.

LBO MODEL

Role: Private equity associate at a top-tier buyout fund with expertise in leveraged transaction modeling.

Task: Build a complete LBO model framework for [COMPANY NAME] at a proposed entry of [ENTRY MULTIPLE]x EBITDA.

Context: [Paste: LTM EBITDA, free cash flow conversion rate, existing debt structure, projected EBITDA growth rate, target exit year (3, 5, or 7). Include known sector debt capacity benchmarks.]

Steps:

1. Structure sources and uses: equity check, senior debt, mezzanine if applicable
2. Build the debt schedule: opening balances, interest expense, amortization, cash sweep
3. Project EBITDA and free cash flow through exit
4. Model exit at entry multiple and at ±1.5x entry multiple
5. Calculate IRR and MOIC at each scenario

Goal: A returns analysis that tells the deal team whether this clears a 20% IRR hurdle at reasonable assumptions.

Constraints: Flag leverage levels exceeding sector norms. Use consistent interest rate assumptions unless instructed otherwise. Do not model synergies unless explicitly provided.

Output: Sources and uses table, debt schedule summary, exit bridge, IRR/MOIC matrix across entry and exit multiple combinations.

Q. How Users Can Apply This Prompt?

Users can apply this prompt by providing the relevant financial and transaction assumptions for the target company. This typically includes last twelve months (LTM) EBITDA, free cash flow conversion rates, the existing debt structure, expected EBITDA growth, and the intended investment horizon, usually three, five, or seven years. Sector-specific debt capacity benchmarks can also be included to ensure that the leverage assumptions remain realistic within the industry context. Once this information is provided, the prompt systematically constructs the LBO framework by first outlining the sources and uses of capital, then building a simplified debt schedule that tracks balances, interest expenses, and amortization over the investment period.

The analysis continues by projecting EBITDA growth and free cash flow generation through the exit year, allowing the model to estimate the value of the company at the time of sale. Exit scenarios are then tested using the entry multiple as well as upside and downside variations, helping to assess how sensitive the investment returns are to market conditions. The final output calculates the internal rate of return (IRR) and multiple of invested capital (MOIC) across different scenarios, presenting the results in a structured format suitable for internal investment discussions. By clearly outlining sources and uses, debt dynamics, and exit outcomes, this framework provides a professional-grade returns analysis that helps determine whether a potential transaction meets the return hurdles typically required by private equity investment committees.

Framework 4

The M&A Accretion–Dilution Analysis Framework

In mergers and acquisitions, one of the most immediate questions asked by executives, investors, and deal committees is whether a proposed transaction will increase or decrease the acquiring company's earnings per share (EPS). This is where Accretion/Dilution Analysis becomes a critical component of financial modeling in investment banking. By comparing the acquirer's standalone earnings with the pro forma earnings of the combined company after the transaction, analysts can determine whether the deal is financially beneficial in the short and medium term. Because public markets often react quickly to changes in earnings expectations, this analysis helps bankers and corporate executives understand how a transaction may be perceived by investors and whether it strengthens the strategic rationale of the acquisition. Running a reliable accretion/dilution analysis requires a structured approach that reflects how M&A bankers at bulge-bracket investment banks evaluate transactions. Analysts must carefully account for the purchase price, funding mix between cash and stock, financing costs, and the impact of operational synergies. In addition, the analysis must consider market valuation metrics such as the acquirer's price-to-earnings multiple when issuing stock as deal consideration.

This prompt is designed to replicate that professional workflow by guiding the user through the core steps of building a pro forma income statement, calculating the combined company's EPS, and determining the degree of accretion or dilution resulting from the transaction. It also introduces scenario analysis around potential synergies, allowing analysts to assess how operational improvements could influence the deal's financial attractiveness.

M&A ACCRETION/DILUTION ANALYSIS

Role: M&A banker at a bulge-bracket firm advising the acquirer on a potential transaction.

Task: Run an accretion/dilution analysis for [ACQUIRER] buying [TARGET] at [PROPOSED PRICE].

Context: [Paste: acquirer's current EPS, net income, shares outstanding, P/E multiple, cost of debt. Target's net income and shares outstanding. Deal mix: % cash vs. % stock.]

Steps:

1. Calculate purchase price and deal consideration by funding mix
2. Build pro forma combined income statement through EPS
3. Calculate accretion/dilution to acquirer EPS in Year 1 and Year 3
4. Model synergies from 0 to [X]% of target revenue in 25% increments
5. Calculate the breakeven synergy level for deal neutrality

Goal: A clear answer to whether this deal is dilutive before synergies, and what synergy achievement makes it compelling.

Constraints: Use acquirer's current P/E for stock consideration, not forward. Separate operating synergies from cost synergies. Flag purchase price premium against sector precedent transactions.

Output: Pro forma EPS bridge, accretion/dilution table by synergy scenario, breakeven synergy analysis, one-paragraph deal rationale.

Q. How Users Can Apply This Prompt?

Users can apply this framework by providing the key financial inputs for both the acquiring company and the target. These inputs typically include the acquirer's current earnings per share, net income, shares outstanding, P/E multiple, and cost of debt, along with the target company's net income and share count. The proposed transaction price and the structure of the deal, specifically the percentage funded with cash versus stock, should also be included. Once these details are provided, the prompt systematically constructs the accretion/dilution analysis by calculating the total purchase price, allocating consideration across the funding mix, and building a simplified pro forma income statement that reflects the combined entity after the transaction.

The framework then measures the impact of the deal on the acquirer's earnings per share in both Year 1 and Year 3, providing insight into the short-term and medium-term financial effects of the acquisition. It also models potential synergies across a range of scenarios, allowing users to determine the level of operational improvement required for the transaction to become accretive. By calculating the breakeven synergy threshold, the model highlights the minimum performance improvements needed for the deal to be earnings-neutral. The final output presents a clear EPS bridge, accretion/dilution tables across synergy scenarios, and a concise deal rationale, delivering a professional-grade M&A analysis similar to the frameworks used by investment banking advisory teams when evaluating strategic acquisitions.

Framework 5

The Sell-Side Equity Research Framework

In institutional finance, equity research reports play a critical role in shaping investment decisions for portfolio managers, hedge funds, and institutional investors. These reports provide a structured analysis of a company's financial performance, competitive positioning, and future growth prospects, ultimately leading to a clear buy, hold, or sell recommendation. An initiation-of-coverage report is particularly significant because it represents the first formal research opinion from an analyst on a company. Such reports must combine rigorous financial modeling with strategic industry insight, presenting a balanced view that highlights both opportunities and risks. When executed properly, an equity research note becomes a valuable decision-making tool that helps investors understand whether a stock is mispriced relative to its underlying fundamentals and growth potential.

Creating a professional equity research initiation note requires more than simply summarizing financial data. Analysts must construct a compelling investment thesis, evaluate valuation through multiple frameworks, and present a structured argument that can withstand scrutiny from institutional investors. This prompt is designed to mirror the workflow used by sell-side equity research analysts at leading investment banks and brokerage firms. It guides the user through identifying the core investment thesis, building a blended valuation using both Discounted Cash Flow (DCF) and trading comparables, and developing scenario-based forecasts that capture potential upside and downside outcomes.

By structuring the analysis around catalysts, risks, and clearly defined assumptions, the prompt ensures that the final research note is analytical, balanced, and aligned with professional equity research standards.

EQUITY RESEARCH NOTE

Role: Sell-side equity research analyst initiating coverage on [COMPANY NAME] in the [SECTOR] space.

Task: Draft a complete initiation-of-coverage note with a buy/hold/sell rating and 12-month price target.

Context: [Paste: recent earnings summary, 3 years of revenue and EBITDA, current share price, market cap, key business segments, 2 known competitors. Include any recent management guidance.]

Steps:

1. Summarize the investment thesis in 3 bullets: why now, what the market is missing, key catalyst
2. Build a blended valuation: DCF + comps target price
3. **Model 3 scenarios:** base, bull, bear - with probability weights
4. Identify 3 upside catalysts and 3 key risks with estimated EPS impact
5. Write a 150-word executive summary in analyst note style

Goal: A note a portfolio manager could use to make a position decision.

Constraints: No buy recommendation without a specific mispriced catalyst. Flag all forward estimates as modeled, not consensus. Distinguish facts from analyst judgment throughout.

Output: Thesis bullets, scenario table, catalyst/risk matrix, price target derivation, 150-word summary.

Q. How Users Can Apply This Prompt?

Users can apply this framework by providing the relevant financial and strategic information about the company being analyzed. This typically includes recent earnings results, three years of historical revenue and EBITDA data, current share price, market capitalization, and a breakdown of key business segments, along with a few notable competitors in the same sector. If available, management guidance and recent strategic developments can also be included to enrich the analysis. Once this information is supplied, the prompt systematically builds the research note by first identifying the core investment thesis, highlighting why the stock is attractive at the current moment, what the market may be overlooking, and what near-term catalysts could drive revaluation.

The framework then develops a blended valuation approach, combining DCF analysis with comparable company multiples to derive a reasonable price target. To capture uncertainty in future performance, the analysis models base, bull, and bear scenarios, each assigned probability weights to estimate the expected valuation range. The prompt also requires analysts to clearly identify key upside catalysts and potential risks, along with their estimated impact on earnings. The final output includes structured thesis points, scenario analysis tables, a catalyst and risk matrix, and a concise executive summary written in the style of a professional analyst note. When supported by reliable data, this framework enables users to produce a comprehensive, institution-quality equity research initiation report suitable for informing portfolio-level investment decisions.

Framework 6
The M&A Due Diligence Framework

In mergers and acquisitions, due diligence is the phase where strategic ambition meets rigorous verification. Before capital is committed and transactions move toward closing, deal teams must thoroughly evaluate the target company's financial health, operational structure, legal obligations, and strategic positioning. A well-structured due diligence process allows investors and advisors to identify risks, validate assumptions behind the acquisition thesis, and uncover opportunities that may influence valuation or deal structure. Because acquisitions often involve significant capital commitments and long-term strategic implications, due diligence must be systematic, disciplined, and focused on the issues that have the greatest potential impact on the success of the transaction.

Executing an effective due diligence process requires coordination across multiple disciplines, including financial analysis, legal review, operational assessment, and commercial evaluation. In professional M&A environments, senior advisors and deal teams organize their diligence workstreams carefully to ensure that critical questions are addressed early in the transaction timeline. This prompt is designed to replicate the structured approach used by M&A advisory teams and private equity investors when evaluating potential acquisitions. Rather than producing a generic checklist, the framework focuses on identifying the most important diligence questions, those that could materially affect the investment decision or alter the deal structure.

By organizing the process into clearly defined workstreams and prioritizing the most impactful questions, the prompt helps ensure that the diligence effort remains focused on value drivers and transaction risks rather than routine information gathering.

M&A DUE DILIGENCE BRIEF

Role: Senior M&A advisor running the buy-side diligence process on [TARGET COMPANY] in [INDUSTRY].

Task: Build a structured due diligence briefing for the deal team and management committee.

Context: [Paste: target's business model, key revenue streams, customer concentration data, last 3 years of financials, and strategic rationale for the acquisition.]

Steps:

1. Map the 5 priority diligence workstreams: financial, commercial, legal, operational, management
2. For each workstream, list the top 5 questions that could change the deal decision
3. Identify 3 deal-breaker risks, those that, if confirmed, kill the transaction
4. Flag key data room items needed per workstream
5. Build a diligence timeline from LOI to close with week-by-week milestones

Goal: A document a deal team picks up on Day 1 and immediately knows where to focus.

Constraints: Distinguish standard diligence items from deal-specific risks. Flag anything requiring third-party expertise (legal, technical, actuarial). Rank questions by potential value impact.

Output: Workstream table, 25 diligence questions ranked by priority, deal-breaker risks section, data room checklist, milestone timeline.

Q. How Users Can Apply This Prompt?

Users can apply this framework by providing key background information about the target company and the strategic rationale for the acquisition. This typically includes details about the target's business model, revenue streams, customer concentration, and historical financial performance over the past three years, along with the strategic objectives behind the proposed transaction.

Once this information is provided, the prompt systematically constructs a structured due diligence briefing that organizes the investigation across five core workstreams: financial, commercial, legal, operational, and management. For each workstream, the framework identifies the most critical questions that could influence the investment decision, ensuring that the deal team focuses on the issues with the highest potential impact.

In addition to identifying priority questions, the framework highlights potential deal-breaker risks, issues that could fundamentally undermine the transaction if confirmed. It also outlines the key documents and information required in the data room for each diligence area, ensuring that the team gathers the necessary evidence to validate assumptions and assess risks. Finally, the prompt builds a clear timeline from the signing of a Letter of Intent (LOI) through the closing of the transaction, outlining week-by-week milestones that help coordinate the work of internal teams and external advisors.

The resulting document provides a structured, professional-grade diligence briefing that allows deal teams and management committees to quickly understand where to focus their attention during the critical early stages of an acquisition process.

Framework 7

The Investment Committee Decision Framework

In private equity and institutional investing, the Investment Committee (IC) memo serves as one of the most critical documents in the decision-making process. Before capital is committed to a transaction, deal teams must present a clear and comprehensive case explaining why the investment opportunity is attractive, how it will generate returns, and what risks must be carefully managed. Unlike lengthy research reports or technical financial models, an IC memo must distill complex analysis into a concise and persuasive narrative that senior partners can quickly evaluate. The goal is not only to present the opportunity but also to demonstrate that the investment team has rigorously examined the company's fundamentals, market dynamics, and potential downside scenarios. As a result, a well-structured IC memo becomes the central document that guides discussion and ultimately determines whether the investment receives approval.

Preparing a strong investment committee memo requires balancing analytical depth with clarity and brevity. Senior partners reviewing investment proposals typically have limited time, and they expect the memo to clearly articulate the core investment thesis, financial returns, and principal risks without unnecessary complexity. This prompt is designed to replicate the structured approach used by private equity partners and deal teams when presenting an opportunity to an investment committee. It guides the user through the essential sections of an IC memo, including the executive summary, business overview, investment thesis, financial return analysis, and risk assessment.

By organizing the information in a logical and disciplined format, the prompt ensures that the final document communicates the full investment case while remaining concise enough to be reviewed in a short meeting or pre-read session.

INVESTMENT COMMITTEE MEMO

Role: Partner at a private equity firm presenting a new investment to the IC.

Task: Write a complete investment committee memo for [DEAL NAME / COMPANY].

Context: [Paste: company description, proposed deal structure, entry price and multiple, projected hold period, thesis summary, and 3–5 key financial metrics.]

Steps:

1. Executive summary: 3-paragraph overview (opportunity, structure, expected returns)
2. Business overview: company, market, competitive position
3. Investment thesis: why now, what creates value, what others are missing
4. Financial summary: entry metrics, return scenarios (base/upside/downside), exit assumptions
5. Risk section: top 5 risks with specific mitigation for each

Goal: A memo a skeptical IC partner can read in 10 minutes and understand the full picture.

Constraints: Every return projection requires stated assumptions. No unsourced market size claims. Risk section must include a scenario that kills the investment.

Output: Full IC memo: executive summary, business overview, investment thesis, financial summary, risk analysis. 600–800 words.

Q. How Users Can Apply This Prompt?

Users can apply this framework by providing the core information related to the potential investment opportunity. This typically includes a description of the target company, the proposed transaction structure, the entry valuation and multiple, the expected investment horizon, and a summary of the key drivers behind the investment thesis. Additional financial metrics, such as revenue growth, EBITDA margins, or projected return scenarios, can also be included to support the analysis. Once this context is provided, the prompt systematically constructs a complete investment committee memo by first summarizing the opportunity, transaction structure, and expected returns in a concise executive overview.

The framework then expands into a structured analysis of the company's business model, market environment, and competitive positioning, helping decision-makers understand the strategic rationale behind the investment. It further outlines the core investment thesis, explaining why the opportunity exists now and what specific factors are expected to drive value creation over the investment period. The financial summary section provides a clear overview of entry metrics, potential return outcomes across multiple scenarios, and the assumptions behind exit valuations. Finally, the memo includes a rigorous risk analysis that highlights the most significant threats to the investment and the strategies proposed to mitigate them.

When used effectively, this framework enables users to produce a clear, professional-grade investment committee memo that communicates the full investment case while allowing decision-makers to evaluate the opportunity efficiently and confidently.

Framework 8

The Client Pitch Strategy Model

In investment banking, the pitch book is one of the most important tools used to communicate strategic ideas to corporate clients and their boards. While financial models and valuation analyses provide the quantitative foundation for a transaction, the narrative within a pitch book is what ultimately persuades decision-makers to consider a particular course of action. Senior executives and board members are not simply reviewing numbers, they are evaluating whether a proposed transaction aligns with the company's strategic objectives, market positioning, and long-term value creation goals. As a result, the narrative portion of a pitch must clearly explain the opportunity, highlight the urgency of action, and demonstrate why the recommended approach represents the most compelling path forward.

Crafting a compelling pitch narrative requires more than summarizing data or listing transaction benefits. In professional advisory environments, senior investment bankers structure their recommendations carefully to ensure that every message resonates with the client's priorities and the concerns of the board. The narrative must present a clear argument: why the current market environment creates an opportunity, why the proposed transaction is strategically superior to alternatives, and how potential risks can be managed through thoughtful execution. This prompt is designed to replicate the approach used by senior investment bankers when preparing boardroom-ready pitch materials.

By guiding the user through key sections such as the "Why Now" argument, strategic rationale, stakeholder messaging, and risk mitigation, the framework ensures that the resulting narrative is persuasive, structured, and aligned with professional advisory standards.

PITCH BOOK NARRATIVE

Role: Senior investment banker preparing the strategic rationale section of a pitch for [CLIENT].

Task: Write the strategic narrative for a pitch recommending [TRANSACTION TYPE: M&A / IPO / Debt Raise / Strategic Review] for [COMPANY NAME].

Context: [Paste: company overview, current situation, proposed transaction structure, key value creation levers, and any specific client priorities or sensitivities.]

Steps:

1. Write the "Why Now" section: 3 market or company factors creating urgency
2. Write the strategic rationale: why this transaction maximizes value vs. alternatives
3. Draft key messages for each stakeholder: board, management, shareholders
4. Summarize execution risks and how the proposed approach mitigates them
5. Propose 3 slide titles that anchor the recommendation narrative

Goal: Persuasive, boardroom-ready copy that tells a clear story, not a feature list.

Constraints: No "transformative" or "synergy-driven" language without specifics. Tailor every message to the client's stated priorities. Avoid jargon a non-finance board member couldn't follow.

Output: 4 narrative sections (Why Now, Strategic Rationale, Stakeholder Messages, Risk Mitigants) plus 3 proposed slide titles with one-line descriptions.

Q. How Users Can Apply This Prompt?

Users can apply this framework by providing key contextual information about the client and the proposed transaction. This typically includes a company overview, the organization's current strategic situation, the structure of the recommended transaction, and the primary drivers of value creation. Any specific client priorities, sensitivities, or strategic goals can also be included to ensure the narrative reflects the company's unique circumstances. Once this information is provided, the prompt systematically develops a strategic pitch narrative beginning with a "Why Now" section that highlights the market conditions or company-specific developments creating urgency for action.

The framework then builds a clear strategic rationale explaining why the proposed transaction, whether it involves a merger, acquisition, public offering, debt raise, or strategic review, maximizes shareholder value compared to other potential options. It also generates tailored messaging for key stakeholders, including the board of directors, management team, and shareholders, ensuring that each audience receives a clear and relevant explanation of the strategy. Finally, the analysis addresses execution risks and outlines how the recommended approach mitigates them, reinforcing confidence in the proposed plan.

The output concludes with suggested slide titles and narrative anchors, helping translate the strategic argument into clear, persuasive pitch book slides suitable for board-level discussions.

Claude as a Market Research Engine

One of the most powerful capabilities of Claude is its ability to function as a high-level market research assistant. When used correctly, it can dramatically accelerate the way analysts, consultants, and financial professionals study industries, competitors, and emerging trends. Many professionals still treat AI tools as simple question-and-answer systems. However, advanced teams use Claude in a much more structured way. Instead of asking random questions, they design prompts that allow Claude to analyze entire markets, extract patterns, and summarize complex information into clear insights. This approach transforms Claude from a basic productivity tool into a research engine capable of supporting institutional-level analysis. Across strategy consulting and investment environments, organizations such as McKinsey & Company, Goldman Sachs, and JPMorgan Chase increasingly rely on AI systems to accelerate research workflows.

While human expertise remains essential, AI dramatically reduces the time required to gather and structure information. The result is a major productivity shift. Research that previously required several days can now be structured within hours.

Building the Market Landscape

The first step in serious market research is understanding the structure of an industry. Analysts typically begin by identifying:

- Market size
- Growth rate
- Key segments
- Major competitors
- Regulatory influences
- Supply chain dynamics

Claude can help assemble this foundational view quickly. By providing a clear prompt, users can generate a structured overview of an industry in seconds. For example, a prompt might ask Claude to map the competitive landscape of a sector, identify the leading companies, and summarize the major growth drivers. The output often provides a clean, organized summary of the market, which can then be refined with additional research. This step allows analysts to move rapidly from information gathering to strategic thinking.

Competitive Analysis

After understanding the overall market structure, the next stage is analyzing competitors. Claude is particularly effective at processing large amounts of qualitative data. This includes materials such as:

- Earnings call transcripts
- Investor presentations
- Annual reports
- Strategic announcements

By reviewing these sources, Claude can identify recurring themes in company strategies. For example, it may highlight how firms are approaching pricing, product development, or geographic expansion. Instead of manually reading hundreds of pages of documents, analysts can ask Claude to extract the most important strategic signals. This allows professionals to focus their attention on interpreting insights rather than searching for them.

Identifying Strategic Patterns

Another major strength of Claude is its ability to identify patterns across companies and industries. Experienced analysts often look for recurring strategic models. For example:

- How successful technology platforms scale revenue
- How financial companies expand into adjacent services
- How high-growth startups capture market share quickly

Claude can compare multiple companies simultaneously and highlight similarities in their strategies. This helps analysts recognize patterns that may indicate long-term competitive advantages or emerging industry trends. For market researchers, this ability to detect patterns can be extremely valuable.

Generating Investment or Strategy Ideas

Once the industry structure and competitive dynamics are understood, Claude can help generate potential strategic or investment ideas. For instance, users may ask Claude to identify:

- Industries with strong growth potential
- Sectors experiencing disruption
- Companies with improving margins
- Markets benefiting from technological change

Claude does not replace detailed financial analysis, but it can help professionals surface interesting opportunities quickly. These ideas can then be tested with deeper financial modeling and traditional research. In many cases, Claude serves as a starting point for hypothesis generation.

Turning Research into Clear Narratives

A final challenge in market research is transforming data into a clear narrative. Consultants, analysts, and bankers often need to present insights in reports, investment memos, or strategic presentations. Claude can assist by helping structure research findings into logical arguments. For example, it can help outline sections such as:

- Market opportunity
- Competitive landscape
- Strategic risks
- Long-term growth drivers

This makes it easier to communicate complex research in a way that decision-makers can quickly understand.

Q. Why the Skill Gap Is So Large?

Although Claude is widely available, the difference between casual users and advanced users is significant. Most people ask simple questions and receive simple answers. High-performing teams, on the other hand, treat Claude like a collaborative research partner. They provide detailed prompts, clear objectives, and structured instructions. As a result, Claude produces more thoughtful and useful outputs. The professionals who learn to guide AI tools effectively will gain a strong advantage in research and analysis.

Claude's true strength lies in its ability to compress large amounts of information into structured insights. When integrated into a research workflow, it can support everything from industry analysis to idea generation. However, the value of the tool ultimately depends on how it is used. The most successful professionals do not rely on AI blindly. Instead, they combine AI-generated insights with human judgment and financial expertise. When used in this balanced way, Claude becomes far more than a simple assistant. It becomes a powerful partner in modern market research.

Framework 1

The TAM–SAM–SOM Market Analysis Framework

Understanding the true size of a market is one of the most important steps in evaluating a new business opportunity, product launch, or investment thesis. Investors, strategy teams, and founders rely on market sizing frameworks, particularly the Total Addressable Market (TAM), Serviceable Available Market (SAM), and Serviceable Obtainable Market (SOM) model, to determine whether a business idea has the scale required to justify capital investment and long-term growth. A well-constructed market sizing analysis goes beyond broad estimates and instead breaks the opportunity down using structured assumptions, clear calculations, and credible data sources. When done correctly, it provides a realistic picture of both the overall market opportunity and the share a company can realistically capture within its target segment.

Market sizing is often presented with overly optimistic assumptions or vague estimates that lack analytical rigor. In professional strategy consulting and market research environments, however, analysts are expected to support every figure with transparent logic and defensible calculations. This prompt is designed to replicate the analytical approach used by senior market research analysts at leading consulting firms such as McKinsey. Rather than simply generating large headline numbers, the framework requires both top-down and bottom-up calculations, ensuring that the market opportunity is validated from multiple perspectives. It also emphasizes the importance of documenting assumptions, identifying areas where estimates are weakest, and benchmarking the results against known industry reports.

By forcing this level of transparency, the prompt helps produce a market sizing analysis that is credible enough for investor presentations, strategy discussions, and board-level decision-making.

Most Founders pay consultants $3K just for a marketing sizing slide. Claude does it in 30s with actual logic:

You are a senior market research analyst at McKinsey. Calculate the TAM, SAM, and SOM for [YOUR PRODUCT/SERVICE] in [TARGET MARKET].

For each:

1. Show your math (top-down AND bottom-up approach)
2. Cite the assumptions you're making
3. Flag where your estimates are weakest
4. Compare to any known market reports if applicable

Format as an investor-ready slide with numbers, not paragraphs. If my market is smaller than I think, tell me now.

Q. How Users Can Apply This Prompt?

Users can apply this framework by providing two key pieces of information: the product or service being analyzed and the target market or geographic region where it will operate. With this context, the prompt guides the analysis through a structured process of estimating the market opportunity. First, it calculates the Total Addressable Market (TAM) by assessing the full demand for the product or service across the entire potential customer base. It then narrows the focus to the Serviceable Available Market (SAM), the portion of the total market that can realistically be served based on product capabilities, distribution channels, or geographic constraints. Finally, the analysis estimates the Serviceable Obtainable Market (SOM), representing the realistic share of the market the company could capture within a defined time horizon.

The framework also requires each estimate to be supported by clear calculations and explicit assumptions, allowing users to understand how the numbers were derived. Any areas of uncertainty or weak assumptions are flagged to ensure transparency, and the results can be compared against published market research reports when available. The final output is structured in a concise, investor-ready slide format, presenting the TAM, SAM, and SOM estimates alongside the logic behind them.

Framework 2

The Data-Driven Customer Persona Framework

Understanding the customer is one of the most critical foundations of successful product development, marketing strategy, and business growth. While many organizations attempt to define their audience through broad demographic categories, truly effective customer insight comes from analyzing behavioral patterns, motivations, and decision-making triggers. This is where structured customer persona frameworks become valuable. When developed correctly, personas help companies move beyond surface-level assumptions and instead build a clear picture of the individuals who actually experience the problem the product is designed to solve. By identifying how customers think, what information they trust, and what ultimately drives their purchasing decisions, businesses can create more effective messaging, product features, and acquisition strategies. Many customer persona exercises fail because they rely on generic descriptions that offer little practical value for strategy or marketing execution. Phrases like "a 35-year-old marketing manager" rarely reveal how a person evaluates solutions, what triggers their search for a product, or what objections may prevent them from making a purchase. In professional research environments, however, analysts focus on behavioral insights rather than demographic stereotypes. This prompt is designed to replicate the analytical mindset used by consumer insights researchers at leading financial and consulting institutions, where the goal is to uncover actionable patterns in how customers identify problems and evaluate solutions.

By structuring personas around triggers, decision processes, objections, and real language used by customers, the framework produces insights that can directly inform product positioning, marketing campaigns, and customer acquisition strategies.

Consultants charge $5K to interview 10 people and hand you a persona deck with stock photos. This is better:

Role: You are a consumer insights researcher at Goldman Sachs

Task: Build 3 detailed customer personas for [YOUR PRODUCT] in [INDUSTRY]

For each persona:

1, Demographics + psychographics (what do they read, follow, trust?)
2. **Buying trigger:** What event makes them Google your solution?
3. **Decision process:** Who else influences their purchase?
4. **Objections:** What's their #1 reason to say no?
5. Exact phrases they'd use to describe their problem (for ad copy)

Constraints:

1. No generic "35-year-old marketing manager" personas
2. Base everything on behavioral patterns, not demographics
3. Each persona should suggest a different acquisition channel

Q. How Users Can Apply This Prompt?

Users can apply this framework by specifying the product or service being analyzed along with the industry or market context in which it operates. With this information, the prompt constructs three distinct customer personas based on behavioral patterns rather than superficial demographic labels. Each persona explores how individuals in the target market discover and evaluate solutions, including the information sources they trust, the events that trigger their search for a product, and the stakeholders who influence their final purchasing decision. The framework also identifies common objections that may prevent adoption and highlights the exact language customers might use when describing their problem, an insight that can be especially valuable for crafting advertising copy and product messaging.

In addition, each persona is designed to suggest a different customer acquisition pathway, helping businesses understand which marketing channels may be most effective for reaching each segment. By connecting customer behavior with specific messaging and distribution strategies, the framework turns persona development into a practical strategic tool rather than a theoretical exercise. The result is a set of structured, insight-driven personas that help organizations better understand their customers and design more effective approaches to product development, marketing, and growth.

Framework 3

The Strategic Competitor Positioning Framework

In highly competitive markets, success rarely depends on building a product in isolation. Instead, companies must clearly understand how their offering compares to existing solutions and where meaningful differentiation can be created. A competitor positioning map is a widely used strategic tool that helps businesses visualize how different players in a market are perceived relative to one another. By mapping competitors along key strategic dimensions, such as price, product sophistication, customer focus, or ease of use, organizations can identify gaps in the competitive landscape that may represent opportunities for differentiation. When supported by real market insights and customer feedback, this type of analysis can reveal where existing solutions fall short and where new entrants or innovative products can establish a stronger market position.

Competitive analysis is often limited to surface-level observations, such as reviewing marketing claims or product feature lists. However, true competitive positioning is determined not by what companies claim about themselves but by how customers actually perceive their products and experiences. This prompt is designed to encourage a deeper level of competitive analysis by focusing on real-world indicators such as pricing models, customer segments served, and recurring complaints or weaknesses identified in public reviews. By incorporating insights from platforms where users openly discuss product experiences, the framework moves beyond theoretical positioning and instead highlights the practical strengths and limitations of each competitor.

This approach mirrors the analytical mindset used by strategy teams and market researchers who seek to understand not only where competitors stand today, but also which opportunities remain underserved in the market.

Don't manually analyze competitors. Dump everything into Claude and get a strategy in minutes:

Analyze these competitors in [INDUSTRY]:
[LIST 5-7 COMPETITORS]

For each:

1. What's their actual positioning? (not what they say, what customers believe)
2. Pricing model + who they're optimized for
3. Biggest weakness based on public reviews (G2, Reddit, Twitter)
4. What customer segment are they ignoring?

Then: Map all competitors on a 2x2 matrix. You pick the two axes that reveal the biggest gap in the market.

Tell me where the white space is and what positioning would let me win it.

Q. How Users Can Apply This Prompt?

Users can apply this framework by first listing five to seven competitors operating within a specific industry or market segment. Once the competitors are identified, the prompt guides the analysis by examining several key aspects of each company's positioning. This includes identifying the actual perception customers hold about the product, analyzing how the company structures its pricing and which customer segments it primarily targets, and evaluating weaknesses based on publicly available customer feedback. The analysis also encourages users to consider which types of customers may be overlooked or underserved by existing solutions.

After evaluating individual competitors, the framework organizes the insights into a two-by-two positioning matrix, where the axes are selected to reveal the most meaningful strategic differences within the market. By visualizing competitors within this structure, users can clearly see clusters of similar offerings as well as areas where few or no competitors currently operate. These gaps often represent potential opportunities for new positioning strategies or product innovations.

Framework 4

The Pricing Intelligence Framework

Pricing is one of the most powerful yet complex levers in building a successful product business, particularly in software and SaaS markets. While product quality and marketing strategies often receive significant attention, pricing decisions ultimately determine how value is captured and how customers perceive the product's position within the market. An effective pricing strategy must carefully balance customer willingness to pay, competitive dynamics, and the long-term revenue model of the company. When designed correctly, pricing can accelerate adoption, increase customer lifetime value, and create a clear pathway for sustainable growth. Poorly structured pricing can limit revenue potential, confuse customers, and reduce the perceived value of an otherwise strong product.

Many companies approach pricing with assumptions rather than structured analysis, often copying competitors or selecting price points based on intuition rather than data-driven reasoning. In professional pricing strategy work, however, consultants and growth strategists rely on established analytical frameworks to determine optimal pricing structures. This prompt is designed to replicate the analytical process used by experienced pricing strategists working with SaaS companies, where the goal is to identify the pricing model that best aligns with customer behavior and product value. By evaluating competitive pricing structures, analyzing customer segments, and applying established pricing research methods such as Van Westendorp and Gabor-Granger logic, the framework encourages a disciplined approach to pricing decisions.

Rather than producing vague recommendations, the prompt aims to generate concrete insights that can guide real-world pricing changes.

Most startups guess their pricing. Consultants charge $10K for pricing research. Claude will do competitive pricing analysis for free:

You are a pricing strategist who has worked with 50+ SaaS companies.

My product: [DESCRIBE PRODUCT + CURRENT PRICING]
Competitors: [LIST COMPETITORS + THEIR PRICING]
Target customer: [WHO]

Analyze:

1. What pricing model fits my market? (per seat, usage-based, flat rate, freemium and WHY)
2. What's my optimal price point? Show the reasoning using Van Westendorp or Gabor-Granger logic
3. What's the #1 pricing mistake I'm probably making?
4. Design a 3-tier pricing table with specific feature gates that maximize upgrade rate

Be specific with dollar amounts. No "it depends" answers.

Q. How Users Can Apply This Prompt?

Users can apply this framework by providing three key inputs: a description of their product and its current pricing model, a list of key competitors along with their pricing structures, and a clear definition of the target customer segment. With this context, the prompt evaluates the competitive landscape and identifies which pricing model, such as per-seat subscriptions, usage-based billing, flat-rate pricing, or freemium structures, best aligns with the market and customer usage patterns. The analysis then estimates an optimal price point using structured reasoning derived from established pricing research approaches, helping users understand how customers may perceive value at different price levels.

In addition to recommending a price range, the framework identifies the most common pricing mistakes companies make when entering or competing in the market, highlighting areas where revenue potential may be unintentionally limited. The prompt also generates a three-tier pricing structure designed to encourage product adoption while creating natural upgrade paths as customers grow or require additional capabilities. By specifying clear feature gates and price levels, the resulting pricing table helps businesses maximize conversion and expansion revenue. The final outcome is a structured, data-informed pricing strategy that helps companies position their product effectively while capturing the full value of the solution they offer.

Framework 5

The Quarterly Industry Intelligence Framework

In rapidly evolving industries, decision-makers must constantly monitor changes in technology, competitive dynamics, capital flows, and customer behavior. Organizations that fail to track these developments often find themselves reacting to market shifts rather than anticipating them. This is why industry intelligence reports are widely used by consulting firms, investment teams, and corporate strategy groups to maintain a clear view of emerging opportunities and risks. A well-structured intelligence brief goes beyond summarizing headlines, it identifies the underlying forces reshaping the market and explains what those developments mean for companies operating within the space. By combining analytical insight with evidence from real market activity, these reports help leaders make informed strategic decisions in uncertain environments. Many industry analyses rely heavily on broad observations or generalized commentary that offers limited strategic value. In professional consulting environments, however, market intelligence must be grounded in verifiable evidence, concrete examples, and clear implications for business strategy.

This prompt is designed to replicate the analytical framework used by senior analysts at top-tier consulting firms when preparing quarterly intelligence briefs for clients or internal strategy teams. Instead of simply listing trends, the framework requires each insight to be supported by data or real-world developments, such as funding activity, mergers and acquisitions, or competitive moves by leading companies. By pairing each insight with a clear explanation of its implications, the prompt ensures that the analysis provides actionable intelligence rather than abstract commentary.

McKinsey sells trend reports for $25K. This prompt generates one that's 80% as good:

Role: You are a senior analyst at a top-tier consulting firm preparing a quarterly intelligence brief

Task:

Create a comprehensive market intelligence report for [INDUSTRY] covering:

1. Top 5 trends reshaping the industry right now (with evidence, not vibes)
2. 3 emerging threats most companies aren't tracking yet
3. What the smartest players are doing differently (name names)
4. Where capital is flowing (recent funding rounds, M&A activity, IPO signals)
5. Your "hot take" prediction for the next 12 months</task>

Format:

1. Executive summary (3 sentences max)
2. Each section: insight + evidence + "so what" implication
3. End with 3 strategic recommendations for a company entering this space

Write like a partner presenting to a C-suite. No filler.

Q. How Users Can Apply This Prompt?

Users can apply this framework by specifying the industry or market sector they want to analyze. Once the industry is defined, the prompt generates a structured intelligence report that examines the most important forces shaping the market in the current period. The analysis begins with an executive summary that highlights the key conclusions in a concise format suitable for senior decision-makers. It then explores major industry trends, identifying the developments that are actively transforming the competitive landscape and providing evidence to support each observation.

The framework also examines emerging risks and overlooked threats that may not yet be widely discussed but could have meaningful strategic implications. In addition, the report highlights how leading companies are responding to industry changes, providing real examples of organizations adapting their strategies to stay competitive. Capital allocation trends, including venture funding, acquisitions, and potential IPO signals, are also analyzed to reveal where investors believe future growth opportunities lie. The report concludes with a forward-looking perspective, including a bold prediction about how the industry may evolve over the next twelve months and a set of strategic recommendations for companies considering entry into the market.

The result is a structured, insight-driven intelligence brief that helps organizations understand not only what is happening in an industry today, but also how they should respond strategically.

Framework 6

The Customer Discovery Interview Framework

Customer interviews are one of the most valuable methods for understanding how people actually experience problems, evaluate solutions, and make purchasing decisions. While surveys and analytics provide useful quantitative signals, direct conversations with customers reveal the context, motivations, and behavioral patterns behind those signals. For product teams, founders, and strategists, these insights are essential for validating assumptions about customer needs before investing heavily in product development or marketing. When conducted effectively, customer interviews can uncover the real "jobs to be done," highlight existing workarounds customers rely on, and reveal the economic value they place on solving a particular problem.

Despite their importance, many customer interviews fail to generate meaningful insights because the questions are poorly designed or unintentionally biased. Leading questions, hypothetical scenarios, and vague prompts often produce polite responses rather than honest feedback. In professional user research environments, experienced researchers structure interviews carefully to focus on observed behavior rather than opinions or predictions. This prompt is designed to replicate the approach used by experienced user research leads who have conducted hundreds of interviews to uncover actionable insights.

By emphasizing behavioral questions, testing specific assumptions, and identifying existing workarounds, the framework ensures that the interview process reveals how customers actually behave rather than what they think they might do in the future.

Bad customer interviews confirm what you already believe. This prompt designs questions that surface real insights:

You are a user research lead who has conducted 500+ customer interviews.

I'm building [PRODUCT] for [TARGET CUSTOMER].

My assumptions:

- [ASSUMPTION 1]
- [ASSUMPTION 2]
- [ASSUMPTION 3]

Design a 15-question customer interview guide that:

1. Tests each assumption WITHOUT leading the witness
2. Uncovers jobs-to-be-done (not feature requests)
3. Reveals their current workaround and what they spend on it
4. Includes 3 "trap" questions that expose if they're being polite instead of honest

For each question, tell me: What am I actually learning from the answer?

No "How would you feel about..." questions. Only behavioral questions.

Q. How Users Can Apply This Prompt?

Users can apply this framework by specifying the product they are developing, the target customer segment, and the key assumptions they currently hold about the problem or solution. These assumptions may relate to customer needs, purchasing behavior, or the way customers currently address the problem. Once this context is provided, the prompt generates a structured customer interview guide consisting of fifteen carefully designed questions. Each question is crafted to explore real behaviors and experiences rather than hypothetical reactions, allowing researchers to gather more reliable insights. The framework also explains the purpose behind each question, clarifying what specific insight the researcher should expect to learn from the response. In addition to testing assumptions, the interview guide is designed to uncover the customer's current workflow, the tools or alternatives they rely on today, and any costs associated with those solutions. The inclusion of strategically designed "trap" questions helps identify when respondents may be offering polite or socially desirable answers rather than genuine feedback.

By combining behavioral questioning with clear research objectives, this framework enables teams to conduct structured, insight-driven customer interviews that reveal the real problems customers face and the opportunities for creating meaningful solutions.

Framework 7

Strategic Go-To-Market Channel Analysis

A successful product launch is rarely determined by the product alone, it is defined by how effectively it reaches the right audience through the right channels. In today's highly competitive landscape, choosing the wrong acquisition channels can result in wasted budget, slow growth, and poor customer acquisition efficiency. Growth teams are no longer judged by activity, but by measurable outcomes such as CAC, scalability, and speed to traction. This makes a structured, analytical approach to channel selection not just valuable, but essential. A well-executed go-to-market channel strategy allows businesses to identify where their target customers already exist, how they can be reached efficiently, and which channels can scale sustainably over time.

Many businesses approach growth with a fragmented strategy—testing multiple channels without a clear framework for prioritization or performance measurement. This often leads to generic tactics like "content marketing" or "social media" without understanding the underlying economics or execution strategy. In contrast, top growth strategists evaluate channels based on cost efficiency, time to results, and scalability, while grounding decisions in expected customer acquisition cost (CAC). This prompt is designed to replicate that level of strategic rigor. It forces a structured evaluation of the top acquisition channels, ranks them based on expected returns, and eliminates vague recommendations by requiring quantifiable scoring and clear reasoning.

Additionally, by identifying overused or inefficient channels within a specific market, the framework helps users avoid crowded and diminishing-return strategies.

Consultants charge $8K for a GTM strategy deck. This prompt builds one that actually prioritizes channels by ROI:

You are a growth strategist who has launched 30+ products.

My product: [PRODUCT DESCRIPTION]
Target customer: [WHO]
Budget: [MONTHLY MARKETING BUDGET]
Current traction: [WHAT YOU HAVE SO FAR]

Analyze the top 8 acquisition channels for my business:

1. Score each channel (1-10) on: cost efficiency, time to results, scalability
2. Rank by expected CAC (show your math)
3. **For the top 3 channels:** Give me the exact playbook for the first 30 days
4. Which channel is everyone in my space using that I should AVOID? Why?

No generic "try content marketing" advice. I want specific tactics with estimated costs and timelines.

Q. How Users Can Apply This Prompt?

Users can start by providing key inputs including their product description, target customer profile, available marketing budget, and current traction. These inputs allow the model to contextualize recommendations based on business stage and resource constraints. Once provided, the prompt delivers a ranked analysis of the most relevant acquisition channels, including scoring across critical dimensions and a clear breakdown of expected CAC using logical assumptions. More importantly, the framework goes beyond strategy into execution by outlining a 30-day, step-by-step playbook for the top three channels, enabling users to move quickly from analysis to action. It also highlights which commonly used channel in their space may be inefficient or oversaturated, helping them avoid unnecessary spend. By combining structured evaluation with actionable execution plans, this framework enables users to make data-driven go-to-market decisions and allocate resources toward channels that offer the highest probability of scalable growth.

Framework 8

Precision Survey Design for Actionable Insights

Surveys remain one of the most widely used tools for gathering customer insights, yet most fail to produce reliable or actionable data. The issue is rarely the tool itself, but rather how the survey is designed. Poorly structured questions, leading language, and an overreliance on opinion-based responses often result in data that looks convincing but lacks real-world validity. In contrast, professionally designed surveys, rooted in behavioral science and statistical rigor, focus on what respondents actually do, not what they claim they might do. When executed correctly, surveys can validate critical business hypotheses, quantify customer preferences, and inform high-stakes decisions such as pricing, positioning, and product development. The gap between amateur and expert survey design is significant. Most surveys unintentionally introduce bias, fail to screen the right audience, or collect responses from disengaged participants who click through without attention. In professional research environments, survey design is approached with precision, every question serves a specific purpose, minimizes bias, and contributes to a clearly defined objective. This prompt is designed to replicate that level of discipline. It ensures that the survey begins by identifying the correct target audience, uses behavioral questioning techniques to improve data reliability, and incorporates advanced elements such as conjoint analysis to assess willingness to pay.

Additionally, by including a built-in quality control mechanism and requiring bias identification for each question, the framework helps maintain the integrity of the data collected.

90% of market research surveys ask garbage questions and get garbage data. This fixes that:

You are a survey methodology expert trained in behavioral science.

Goal: I need to validate [SPECIFIC HYPOTHESIS] about [TARGET MARKET]

Design a 12-question survey that:

1. Screens for my actual target customer in the first 2 questions
2. Uses behavioral questions (what they DO) not opinion questions (what they THINK)
3. Includes 1 conjoint analysis question to test willingness to pay
4. Has 1 trick question to filter out people clicking randomly
5. Takes under 4 minutes to complete

For each question:

1. Show the question + answer options
2. Explain what insight it gives me
3. Flag potential bias in the question

Also: What sample size do I need for statistical significance at 95% confidence?

Q. How Users Can Apply This Prompt?

Users can apply this framework by clearly defining the specific hypothesis they want to validate and the target market they are studying. These inputs allow the survey to be tailored to a precise research objective rather than generating generic insights. Once provided, the prompt generates a structured 12-question survey that is optimized for both speed and depth, ensuring it can be completed in under four minutes while still delivering meaningful data.

Each question is presented alongside its intended insight and any potential sources of bias, enabling users to understand not just what they are asking, but why it matters. The inclusion of a conjoint analysis question provides a data-driven way to evaluate pricing sensitivity, while a carefully designed attention check helps filter out low-quality responses. Finally, the framework addresses the often-overlooked aspect of statistical validity by guiding users on the appropriate sample size required to achieve 95% confidence. Altogether, this prompt enables users to design surveys that are methodologically sound, insight-driven, and decision-ready, making them far more effective than traditional, opinion-based questionnaires.

Framework 9

Decision-Driven SWOT Analysis Model

SWOT analysis is one of the most widely used strategic tools in business, yet in many cases, it fails to deliver meaningful outcomes. Too often, it becomes a static exercise, filled with generic observations that neither challenge assumptions nor guide decision-making. In high-performance environments such as investment banking and corporate strategy, however, SWOT is not treated as a checklist, but as a decision-making framework that directly informs competitive positioning and capital allocation. When approached with the right level of rigor, it can uncover defensible advantages, expose critical vulnerabilities, and identify time-sensitive opportunities that demand immediate action.

The key limitation of traditional SWOT analysis lies in its lack of specificity and strategic intent. Vague statements like "strong brand" or "intense competition" do little to help leadership teams make informed decisions. In contrast, experienced strategists focus on what is truly defensible, what is genuinely at risk, and what is changing in the market right now. This prompt is designed to bring that level of clarity and precision into the analysis. By reframing each quadrant with sharper, more demanding questions, such as identifying strengths that competitors cannot replicate in the near term or threats that could realistically disrupt the business, it forces a deeper, more honest evaluation.

Additionally, the inclusion of a 2x2 action matrix transforms the analysis from insight into execution. Rather than stopping at observation, the framework connects strengths to opportunities to define offensive "attack moves," while aligning weaknesses with threats to highlight critical "survival moves". This ensures that the output is not just descriptive, but strategically actionable.

Traditional SWOT is a box-filling exercise that changes nothing. This prompt turns it into a strategy weapon:

You are a corporate strategist at JP Morgan advising on competitive positioning.

Company: [YOUR COMPANY]
Industry: [INDUSTRY]
Top 3 competitors: [LIST THEM]

Run a SWOT analysis, but make it useful:

1. **STRENGTHS:** What do we do that competitors literally cannot copy in the next 12 months?
2. **WEAKNESSES:** What's the honest reason customers choose competitors over us?
3. **OPPORTUNITIES:** What market shift is happening RIGHT NOW that we're not exploiting?
4. **THREATS:** What could put us out of business in 2 years? (not generic "competition", specific scenarios)

Then: Create a 2x2 action matrix:

1. Strengths × Opportunities = Attack moves
2. Weaknesses × Threats = Survival moves

End with: "If I could only do ONE thing this quarter, it should be ___" and defend it.

Q. How Users Can Apply This Prompt?

Users can apply this framework by providing key inputs, including their company, industry, and primary competitors. These inputs ground the analysis in a real competitive context, allowing the framework to generate insights that are both relevant and specific. Once applied, the prompt produces a focused SWOT analysis that goes beyond surface-level observations, highlighting the true drivers of competitive advantage and risk. The structured output then translates these insights into a clear set of strategic actions through the 2x2 matrix, helping users prioritize where to invest time and resources. Finally, by forcing a single, high-conviction recommendation, what should be done this quarter, it ensures that the analysis culminates in a decisive and actionable strategic direction. This makes the framework particularly valuable for founders, operators, and strategy teams who need clarity in environments where speed and precision are critical.

Framework 10

Market Entry Strategy & Feasibility Framework

Entering a new market, whether defined by geography, customer segment, or product category, is one of the most consequential decisions a business can make. While expansion presents opportunities for growth and diversification, it also introduces significant uncertainty, capital risk, and operational complexity. Many market entry efforts fail not because the opportunity didn't exist, but because the decision was driven by optimism rather than rigorous analysis. In professional consulting environments, market entry is evaluated through a structured feasibility lens, balancing market potential with a company's actual ability to compete and win. A disciplined approach ensures that expansion decisions are grounded in reality, not ambition alone.

Traditional market entry analyses often focus heavily on market size and growth, while underestimating critical factors such as competitive intensity, barriers to entry, and internal capability gaps. This creates a dangerous bias toward "greenlighting" expansion without fully understanding execution risk. This prompt is designed to counter that bias by introducing a decision-first framework that evaluates not only whether a market is attractive, but whether the company has a genuine right to win within it. By combining quantitative scoring (market attractiveness) with qualitative judgment (credibility, barriers, and required capabilities), the framework mirrors how experienced consultants assess expansion opportunities. It also introduces often-overlooked elements such as realistic break-even timelines and clearly defined kill criteria, ensuring that users think beyond entry and consider what success and failure actually look like. Importantly, the prompt encourages intellectual honesty by explicitly allowing for the conclusion that the opportunity may not be viable.

Before burning $50K entering a new market, run this:

You are a market entry consultant who has advised Fortune 500 companies on expansion.

We want to enter [NEW MARKET/GEOGRAPHY/SEGMENT].

Our current business: [DESCRIBE]
Our advantages: [WHAT WE BRING]
Our budget: [AVAILABLE INVESTMENT]

Conduct a feasibility analysis:

1. Market attractiveness score (1-10): size, growth rate, profitability, competitive intensity
2. **Our right to win:** What specifically makes us credible in this market? (be honest if the answer is "nothing")
3. Top 3 barriers to entry and cost to overcome each
4. Required partnerships or capabilities we don't have
5. Break-even timeline with realistic assumptions (not best-case fantasy)
6. **Kill criteria:** What signals should make us STOP and exit?

If this is a bad idea, say so. I'd rather hear it from you than from my P&L.

Q. How Users Can Apply This Prompt?

Users can apply this framework by providing a clear description of the target market they intend to enter, along with an overview of their current business, competitive advantages, and available investment budget. These inputs allow the analysis to be tailored to both the opportunity and the organization's capabilities. Once applied, the prompt delivers a structured feasibility assessment that evaluates market attractiveness, identifies the company's true competitive positioning, and highlights the most critical barriers to entry along with the cost and effort required to overcome them.

The framework also surfaces gaps in capabilities and partnerships, helping users understand what must be built or acquired before entering the market. By incorporating a grounded break-even analysis, it sets realistic expectations around timelines and capital deployment. Finally, the inclusion of explicit exit signals ensures that users define in advance the conditions under which the strategy should be reconsidered or abandoned. Altogether, this approach enables decision-makers to pursue expansion with clarity, discipline, and a strong understanding of both upside potential and downside risk.

The Buffett-Style Stock Analysis

One of the most meaningful developments in modern investing is the growing ability to apply disciplined, long-term investment principles, once associated with legendary investors such as Warren Buffett, without requiring decades of experience or access to institutional research teams. Claude enables this shift by acting as a structured financial thinking partner. Rather than replacing expertise, it enhances the way individuals approach stock analysis by bringing clarity, organization, and consistency to the process. It allows users to break down complex businesses, evaluate fundamentals, and form reasoned investment views in a way that is both practical and scalable. As a result, stock analysis evolves from a fragmented and time-intensive task into a repeatable, structured workflow grounded in sound investment principles.

A common trap in investing is the overemphasis on short-term price movements. Many market participants focus on charts, trends, and daily fluctuations, often losing sight of what truly drives long-term returns: the underlying business. The philosophy followed by Warren Buffett takes a fundamentally different approach. It emphasizes understanding the company itself, how it operates, how it generates revenue, and how it sustains growth over time. Claude reinforces this mindset by helping users analyze businesses across key dimensions, including:

- Revenue growth and consistency
- Profitability and margin trends
- Competitive positioning within the industry
- Quality of management decisions
- Long-term strategic direction

Instead of presenting isolated data points, Claude organizes this information into a coherent and structured view of the business. This enables users to move beyond surface-level observations and develop a deeper understanding of how a company creates value. This transition, from focusing on stock prices to focusing on business fundamentals, is a critical step toward more disciplined investing.

Interpreting Financial Statements with Clarity

Financial statements are essential tools for evaluating a company, yet they are often perceived as complex and difficult to interpret. Claude simplifies this process by breaking down the three core financial statements into clear, understandable insights:

Income Statement: Explains how the company generates profits, highlighting revenue, expenses, and net income trends.

Balance Sheet: Provides a snapshot of financial health by outlining assets, liabilities, and shareholder equity.

Cash Flow Statement: Reveals how cash moves through the business, offering insight into operational strength and sustainability.

Beyond simple explanations, Claude can analyze financial data over time to identify meaningful patterns, such as:

- Improving or deteriorating profit margins
- Increasing debt levels or strengthening balance sheets
- Consistency and quality of cash generation

This allows users to quickly assess whether a company is financially stable, improving, or under pressure, without needing to manually interpret every line item.

Framework 1

Institutional-Grade Equity Analysis Framework

In professional investing, a complete stock analysis goes far beyond tracking price movements or reviewing headline financial metrics. Institutional investors such as hedge funds, asset managers, and investment banks, evaluate companies through a comprehensive lens that combines business fundamentals, competitive positioning, financial strength, and valuation discipline. The goal is not simply to understand what a company does, but to determine whether its stock is mispriced relative to its intrinsic value and future potential. This requires a structured, multi-dimensional approach that integrates qualitative insights with quantitative analysis, ultimately leading to a clear and actionable investment view.

Many stock analyses fall short because they focus on isolated aspects, such as earnings growth or valuation multiples—without connecting them into a cohesive investment thesis. In contrast, professional equity research follows a systematic framework that moves from understanding the business model to evaluating competitive advantages, assessing financial performance, identifying risks, and finally forming a valuation-driven conclusion. This prompt is designed to replicate the workflow used by senior Wall Street equity research analysts, ensuring that every key dimension of the investment decision is addressed.

By requiring scenario analysis across bull, base, and bear cases, and enforcing explicit conclusions backed by data or logical reasoning, the framework avoids vague or non-committal outputs and instead delivers a clear, defensible investment perspective.

FULL STOCK ANALYSIS

ROLE: Act as a senior Wall Street equity research analyst who produces institutional-grade stock reports.

TASK: Deliver a complete stock analysis covering every dimension a professional investor evaluates.

STEPS:

1. Ask for ticker and investment horizon before starting
2. Break down business model and revenue streams
3. Evaluate competitive moat and financial health
4. Identify key risks ranked by probability and impact
5. Compare valuation against competitors
6. Build bull, base, and bear scenarios with 12-24 month outlook

RULES:

1. Every claim backed by data or logical argument
2. Valuation conclusion must be explicit — not "it depends"
3. Bull and bear cases must use different assumptions

OUTPUT:

Business → Moat → Financials → Risks → Valuation → Bull / Base / Bear → Outlook

Q. How Users Can Apply This Prompt?

Users can apply this framework by first providing the stock ticker and their investment horizon, which helps tailor the analysis to their specific objectives, whether short-term positioning or long-term investment. Once these inputs are defined, the prompt systematically constructs a full equity research report, beginning with a breakdown of the company's business model and revenue drivers. It then evaluates the company's competitive moat and financial health, providing insight into both its strengths and potential vulnerabilities. The analysis continues by identifying and ranking key risks based on their likelihood and potential impact, ensuring that downside scenarios are thoroughly considered. Valuation is then assessed relative to comparable companies, helping determine whether the stock is overvalued, fairly priced, or undervalued in the current market. Finally, the framework develops bull, base, and bear case scenarios with clearly differentiated assumptions, offering a forward-looking view of potential outcomes over a 12–24 month horizon.

The result is a structured, institutional-grade stock analysis that enables investors to make informed, high-conviction decisions grounded in both analysis and strategic perspective.

Framework 2

The Financial Diagnostics Framework

In financial analysis, understanding a company's true performance requires more than reviewing a single year of results or focusing on headline metrics. Professional investors and analysts evaluate businesses over multiple years to identify underlying trends, consistency of performance, and signs of financial strength or deterioration. This longitudinal approach helps distinguish between companies that are genuinely improving and those that may be masking weaknesses through short-term adjustments. By analyzing key indicators such as revenue growth, profitability, cash flow generation, leverage, and returns on equity over a sustained period, analysts can form a clear view of a company's financial trajectory and long-term viability. Many financial reviews fail because they rely too heavily on isolated data points rather than identifying meaningful trends. A single year of strong earnings, for example, may not reflect the broader financial reality if cash flows are weak or debt levels are rising. In professional settings, forensic financial analysts prioritize trend analysis and cash flow integrity over surface-level metrics. This prompt is designed to replicate that disciplined approach by focusing on five years of financial data and emphasizing the importance of free cash flow as a core indicator of financial health.

By structuring the analysis across revenue, net income, cash flow, margins, debt, and return on equity, the framework ensures a comprehensive evaluation of both operational performance and financial stability. It also enforces a clear and decisive outcome, requiring the analyst to classify the company's financial condition as strong, stable, weakening, or deteriorating, eliminating ambiguity and forcing a definitive, decision-oriented conclusion.

FINANCIAL DIAGNOSTICS FRAMEWORK

ROLE: Act as a forensic financial analyst who reads 5 years of financials to determine if a company is strengthening or deteriorating.

TASK: Break down the last 5 years of financials and deliver a clear health verdict.

STEPS:

1. Ask for ticker before starting
2. Analyze revenue growth, net income trends, and free cash flow
3. Examine margins, debt levels, and return on equity
4. **Deliver verdict:** strong, stable, weakening, or deteriorating

RULES:

1. Trends matter more than single-year snapshots
2. Free cash flow is the truth, revenue can be managed
3. Verdict must be direct, no "it's complicated"

OUTPUT:

Revenue → Net Income → FCF → Margins → Debt → ROE → Health Verdict

Q. How Users Can Apply This Prompt?

Users can apply this framework by providing the stock ticker or company name, which allows the analysis to be anchored in real financial data. Once the company is identified, the prompt systematically evaluates the last five years of financial performance, focusing on trends rather than one-off results. It begins by assessing revenue growth and profitability patterns, then examines free cash flow to determine whether the company is generating sustainable cash or relying on accounting-driven earnings. The analysis continues by reviewing operating margins, debt levels, and return on equity to understand efficiency, financial leverage, and capital effectiveness. Each section contributes to a broader understanding of whether the company's financial position is improving, stable, or deteriorating over time. The final output delivers a clear health verdict, providing users with a straightforward assessment that can inform investment decisions, risk evaluation, or further research. This structured approach enables users to move beyond surface-level analysis and gain a deeper, trend-driven understanding of a company's financial condition.

Framework 3

The Competitive Moat Evaluation Framework

In long-term investing and strategic analysis, a company's success is rarely determined by short-term performance alone. Instead, what truly drives sustained value creation is the strength and durability of its competitive moat, the set of advantages that protect it from competitors and allow it to maintain superior profitability over time. These advantages may take the form of strong brand recognition, network effects, high switching costs, cost leadership, or proprietary technology. However, moats are not static. They can strengthen, weaken, or disappear entirely as markets evolve and competitors adapt. As a result, evaluating not just the presence of a moat, but its durability and trajectory, is essential for making informed investment and strategic decisions.

Traditional moat analysis often stops at identifying advantages without rigorously testing how defensible they are or how they compare against competitors. In professional competitive intelligence and investment research, analysts go further by systematically assessing each dimension of a company's moat and benchmarking it against key rivals. This prompt is designed to replicate that structured approach by breaking the analysis into five core dimensions, brand strength, network effects, switching costs, cost advantages, and intellectual property. By requiring direct comparison with top competitors using the same criteria, the framework ensures that the evaluation is relative, not absolute, which is critical in competitive markets. Additionally, it emphasizes the importance of identifying erosion risk, ensuring that high current scores do not mask underlying weaknesses. The final rating is not just a number but a defensible conclusion supported by clear reasoning, reflecting the standards used by professional analysts and investors.

THE MOAT ANALYSIS

ROLE: Act as a competitive intelligence analyst who evaluates whether a company's advantages are durable, eroding, or already gone.

TASK: Evaluate the competitive moat across five dimensions and rate it against top competitors.

STEPS:

1. Ask for company and top competitors before starting
2. Rate brand strength, network effects, switching costs, cost advantages, and patents
3. Compare ratings against top 2-3 competitors
4. Assign overall moat rating 1-10 with justification

RULES:

1. Eroding moat gets flagged even if score is still high
2. Competitor comparison must use identical criteria
3. Rating must be defensible, show the reasoning

OUTPUT:

5 Moat Dimensions → Competitor Table → Moat Rating (1-10) → Durability Assessment

Q. How Users Can Apply This Prompt?

Users can apply this framework by specifying the company they want to analyze along with its top competitors, ideally two to three key players in the same market. These inputs allow the analysis to be grounded in a real competitive landscape. Once provided, the prompt evaluates each company across the five core moat dimensions, assigning ratings based on observable factors and logical reasoning. The framework then organizes these evaluations into a structured comparison table, making it easy to see where the company stands relative to its competitors. This side-by-side analysis highlights areas of strength as well as vulnerabilities that may not be obvious when viewed in isolation. The final output includes an overall moat rating on a scale of 1 to 10, along with a durability assessment that indicates whether the company's competitive advantages are strengthening, stable, or eroding. By combining structured scoring with comparative analysis and forward-looking judgment, this framework enables users to develop a clear, professional-grade understanding of a company's competitive positioning and long-term defensibility.

Framework 4

Strategic Stock Valuation & Pricing Model

Valuation lies at the core of every investment decision. While market prices reflect current sentiment, they do not always represent a company's true intrinsic value. Professional investors and investment bankers rely on structured valuation frameworks to determine whether a stock is undervalued, fairly priced, or overvalued based on fundamentals rather than market noise. This process involves combining multiple analytical approaches, such as relative valuation and discounted cash flow analysis, to build a well-rounded perspective. By integrating both market-based comparisons and intrinsic value estimation, analysts can arrive at a defensible price range that guides investment decisions with greater precision and confidence.

Many valuation exercises rely too heavily on a single method, such as price-to-earnings multiples or simplified discounted cash flow models, which can lead to incomplete or biased conclusions. In professional investment banking and equity research, valuation is approached as a multi-method discipline, where different techniques are used together to cross-validate results. This prompt is designed to reflect that standard by combining relative valuation (P/E and industry multiples) with intrinsic valuation (DCF analysis). It also enforces analytical rigor by requiring explicit assumptions, highlighting when conclusions depend on overly optimistic scenarios, and producing a clear, non-ambiguous valuation verdict. By mandating a price target range rather than a single-point estimate, the framework acknowledges uncertainty while still delivering actionable guidance. This structured approach ensures that the final output is not just analytical, but also practically useful for decision-making.

THE STOCK VALUATION ANALYSIS

ROLE: Act as an investment banking analyst who determines whether a stock is worth buying at its current price.

TASK: Run a full valuation analysis and deliver a clear undervalued or overvalued conclusion.

STEPS:

1. Ask for ticker and current price before starting
2. Calculate P/E ratio vs. industry average and competitors
3. Build DCF estimate with stated assumptions
4. Pull industry multiples and deliver a price target range

RULES:

1. No single method gets the final word, weight all methods
2. Flag if valuation only works under optimistic assumptions
3. Must include a price target range, not just a direction

OUTPUT:

P/E → DCF → Industry Multiples → Valuation Verdict → Price Target Range

Q. How Users Can Apply This Prompt?

Users can apply this framework by providing the stock ticker and its current market price, which serve as the foundation for the valuation analysis. Once these inputs are defined, the prompt systematically evaluates the stock using multiple methodologies. It begins by comparing the company's price-to-earnings ratio against industry averages and key competitors to assess relative valuation. The analysis then builds a discounted cash flow (DCF) model, incorporating clearly stated assumptions about growth, margins, and discount rates to estimate intrinsic value. In parallel, it examines industry valuation multiples to establish a market-based price range. These methods are then weighted together to produce a balanced valuation view.

Framework 5

The Investment Risk Diagnostics Framework

In investing, understanding potential upside is only half the equation, the other half lies in identifying and managing downside risk. Professional investors recognize that capital is not lost through missed opportunities, but through unanticipated risks that materially impact business performance or permanently impair value. As a result, rigorous risk analysis is a foundational component of institutional investment processes. By systematically evaluating threats across macroeconomic conditions, competitive dynamics, regulatory environments, and company-specific financial risks, analysts can build a clearer picture of what could go wrong and how severe those outcomes may be. Many risk assessments fail because they rely on generic statements or fail to prioritize risks based on their true significance. In professional environments such as investment banking, asset management, and hedge funds, risk analysis is approached with precision and prioritization, focusing only on threats that could meaningfully affect investment outcomes. This prompt is designed to replicate that disciplined approach by requiring risks to be specific, ranked, and evaluated across both probability and impact. A key differentiator of this framework is its focus on permanent capital impairment, situations where an investment could suffer irreversible loss.

By explicitly identifying and flagging these risks, the framework ensures that users pay attention to scenarios that could fundamentally undermine the investment thesis, regardless of how likely they may appear. This structured methodology transforms risk analysis from a checklist into a decision-critical tool.

THE INVESTMENT RISK ANALYSIS

ROLE: Act as a risk analyst who identifies and ranks every material threat before capital is committed.

TASK: Identify the biggest risks and rank them from most to least dangerous.

STEPS:

1. Ask for company and investment thesis before starting
2. Identify risks across macro, disruption, competition, regulation, and finances
3. Rank by probability and impact
4. Flag any permanent capital impairment risk separately

RULES:

1. Risks must be specific, no generic boilerplate
2. Ranking must weigh both probability and severity
3. Permanent impairment risks flagged regardless of probability

OUTPUT:

Risk Categories → Probability + Impact Ranking → Permanent Impairment Flags

Q. How Users Can Apply This Prompt?

Users can apply this framework by providing two essential inputs: the company they are evaluating and their investment thesis. The thesis is particularly important, as it defines the assumptions that the risk analysis will challenge. Once these inputs are established, the prompt systematically identifies risks across key categories, including macroeconomic factors, industry disruption, competitive pressures, regulatory developments, and financial vulnerabilities. Each risk is then assessed and ranked based on its probability of occurrence and potential impact, allowing users to clearly distinguish between minor concerns and critical threats.

The framework also highlights any risks that could lead to permanent capital impairment, ensuring that these high-stakes scenarios are not overlooked. The final output presents a structured and prioritized view of risk, enabling investors to make more informed decisions and determine whether the potential return justifies the level of risk involved. This approach provides a clear, professional-grade risk assessment that supports disciplined capital allocation and long-term investment success.

Framework 6

The Growth Trajectory Analysis Framework

Evaluating a company's growth potential is central to understanding its long-term value. While historical performance provides useful context, professional investors focus on whether a company's future opportunity set is meaningfully larger than its current position. This requires analyzing not just financial trends, but also the size of the addressable market, the company's ability to expand within it, the strength of its product pipeline, and the role of technology in sustaining growth. A structured growth analysis helps determine whether a business can scale over time or whether its growth prospects are already largely priced into the market.

Many growth assessments rely on overly optimistic assumptions or broad market narratives that lack analytical rigor. In professional growth equity and venture investing, however, future potential is evaluated through a combination of market sizing, competitive positioning, and execution capability. This prompt is designed to replicate that disciplined approach by requiring a clear breakdown of growth drivers across market, product, and technology dimensions. It also enforces accountability by distinguishing between sourced data and estimates, ensuring that assumptions are transparent and defensible. Additionally, by requiring three distinct growth scenarios: low, mid, and high, the framework avoids single-path thinking and instead reflects the range of possible outcomes.

This scenario-based approach allows users to understand both upside potential and downside risk, making the analysis more robust and decision-oriented.

THE GROWTH POTENTIAL ANALYSIS

ROLE: Act as a growth equity analyst who evaluates whether a company's future is bigger than its present.

TASK: Analyze future growth potential over 5-10 years across market, product, and technology dimensions.

STEPS:

1. Ask for company and current market position before starting
2. Size total addressable market and industry growth rate
3. Evaluate expansion opportunities, product pipeline, and tech advantages
4. Build low, mid, and high growth scenarios

RULES:

1. Market size claims must be sourced or labeled as estimates
2. Tech advantage only counts if it creates measurable defensibility
3. All three scenarios must use different assumptions

OUTPUT:

Market Size → Expansion → Pipeline → Tech → 3 Growth Scenarios

Q. How Users Can Apply This Prompt?

Users can apply this framework by providing the company name and its current market position, which establishes the baseline for evaluating future growth. Once these inputs are defined, the prompt systematically analyzes the company's potential across several key areas. It begins by estimating the total addressable market (TAM) and industry growth rate, providing context for how large the opportunity could become. The framework then evaluates the company's ability to capture that opportunity through expansion strategies, such as entering new markets, launching new products, or increasing penetration within existing segments. It also assesses the strength of the product pipeline and the extent to which technological advantages contribute to sustainable growth. Finally, the analysis develops three distinct growth scenarios, each based on different assumptions, to provide a realistic range of potential outcomes over a 5–10 year horizon. The result is a structured, forward-looking growth analysis that helps investors and decision-makers assess whether a company has the capacity to deliver meaningful long-term expansion and justify its valuation.

Framework 7

The Institutional Investment Lens

Institutional investors such as hedge funds, asset managers, and pension funds, approach stock selection with a level of rigor that goes far beyond traditional analysis. Their decisions are driven not only by valuation or growth prospects, but by how a stock fits within a broader portfolio strategy, the clarity of its investment thesis, and the presence of identifiable catalysts that can unlock value over time. Unlike retail investing approaches, institutional capital is deployed with a focus on risk-adjusted returns, capital allocation discipline, and conviction-backed position sizing. As a result, understanding how "smart money" evaluates a stock provides valuable insight into whether it has the characteristics required to attract and sustain long-term institutional interest.

Many stock analyses focus on what a company does well but fail to address why large, sophisticated investors would allocate capital to it, or choose to avoid it altogether. In professional investing environments, decisions are shaped by a clear investment thesis, time-bound catalysts, and a balanced view of both upside and downside risks. This prompt is designed to replicate the decision-making framework used by hedge fund portfolio managers, where every position must justify its place within a portfolio. By requiring explicit buy and avoid reasons, the framework ensures that the analysis remains balanced and intellectually honest. The inclusion of catalyst timelines adds a critical dimension often overlooked in basic analysis, emphasizing not just what could drive value, but when.

Finally, by incorporating position sizing logic, the prompt moves beyond binary buy/sell conclusions and instead reflects how institutional investors think in terms of portfolio construction and capital allocation.

THE INSTITUTIONAL INVESTMENT LENS

ROLE: Act as a hedge fund portfolio manager evaluating whether a stock deserves a long-term institutional position.

TASK: Evaluate a stock from an institutional lens — why smart money buys and why they might avoid it.

STEPS:

1. Ask for ticker and market cap before starting
2. Build core investment thesis and identify catalysts with timelines
3. List institutional buy reasons and avoid reasons
4. Deliver portfolio fit verdict with position sizing logic

RULES:

1. Thesis must be specific, not "it's a good company"
2. Catalysts must have a timeline, vague catalysts don't count
3. Verdict must include position sizing logic

OUTPUT:

Thesis → Catalysts → Buy Reasons → Avoid Reasons → Portfolio Fit Verdict

Q. How Users Can Apply This Prompt?

Users can apply this framework by providing the stock ticker and market capitalization, which help contextualize the company within the broader market and investment universe. Once these inputs are defined, the prompt constructs a structured analysis beginning with a clear and specific investment thesis that outlines why the stock may represent an attractive opportunity. The framework then identifies key catalysts, such as earnings inflection points, product launches, regulatory changes, or strategic initiatives, along with realistic timelines for when these events may impact valuation. It proceeds to outline both the reasons institutional investors might build a position in the stock and the factors that could lead them to avoid it, ensuring a balanced evaluation. Finally, the analysis concludes with a portfolio fit verdict, including decisions, recommended position sizing based on conviction, risk profile, and potential return. This enables users to think not just about whether to invest, but how much to allocate and why. The result is a professional, buy-side perspective that mirrors how institutional investors evaluate opportunities and make capital allocation

Framework 8

Long vs. Short Investment Thesis Framework

In professional investing, the ability to evaluate both sides of an argument is critical to making high-conviction decisions. Markets are inherently driven by differing perspectives, what one investor views as an opportunity, another may see as a risk. This is why top hedge funds and investment firms often encourage structured internal debates, where bullish and bearish viewpoints are rigorously tested against each other using data, not sentiment. By challenging assumptions and stress-testing investment theses, this approach helps uncover blind spots and ensures that decisions are grounded in evidence-based reasoning rather than bias or narrative. Many investment analyses suffer from confirmation bias, where only supporting evidence is highlighted while opposing viewpoints are ignored or dismissed. In contrast, professional investors deliberately seek out opposing arguments to strengthen their understanding of a position. This prompt is designed to replicate that discipline by structuring a formal bull vs. bear debate, where both sides are required to present data-backed arguments and directly engage with each other's strongest points.

The framework enforces accountability by requiring rebuttals that address specific arguments rather than introducing unrelated points. It also introduces a scoring mechanism, ensuring that the debate leads to a clear, decisive outcome rather than an ambiguous conclusion. By forcing one side to "win," the prompt mirrors real-world investment decision-making, where capital must ultimately be allocated based on the strength of conviction.

THE BULL VS BEAR DEBATE

ROLE: Act as a debate moderator hosting two analysts — one bullish, one bearish, both arguing with data not sentiment.

TASK: Run a structured bull vs. bear debate and deliver a conclusion based on argument strength.

STEPS:

1. Ask for ticker and current price before starting
2. Bull presents 3 data-backed arguments, bear presents 3 counterarguments
3. Each side rebuts the other's strongest point
4. Score arguments and declare a winner

RULES:

1. No opinion without data, both sides
2. Rebuttals must engage with the actual argument
3. One side must win, no "both have merit" conclusions

OUTPUT: Bull Case → Bear Case → Rebuttals → Scorecard → Conclusion

Q. How Users Can Apply This Prompt?

Users can apply this framework by providing the stock ticker and its current market price, which establish the context for the debate. Once these inputs are defined, the prompt simulates a structured discussion between two analysts, one presenting the bullish case and the other presenting the bearish perspective. Each side develops three data-backed arguments, ensuring that the analysis is grounded in measurable factors such as financial performance, valuation metrics, or industry trends. The debate then progresses to rebuttals, where each side directly challenges the most compelling argument presented by the other. This step is critical, as it tests the robustness of each thesis under scrutiny. The framework concludes with a scorecard that evaluates the strength of the arguments, followed by a final decision declaring a winner based on the evidence presented.

By combining structured argumentation with data-driven evaluation, this framework enables users to gain a balanced and deeply tested perspective on an investment opportunity, helping them make more informed and confident decisions.

Claude and the $15,000 Legal Rewrite: Contracts Without the $800/Hour Barrier

The rules of leverage have quietly been rewritten. For decades, access to high-quality legal work has been gated behind intimidating hourly rates, opaque processes, and long back-and-forth cycles with corporate law firms. Founders, freelancers, and creators have historically faced a frustrating trade-off: either spend thousands of dollars for precision and protection, or cut corners with generic templates that rarely fit the nuances of real-world situations. That paradigm is shifting, rapidly.

Today, tools like Claude are no longer just assistants; they are evolving into highly capable drafting partners that can interpret intent, structure complex agreements, and produce documents that mirror the clarity and rigor once expected only from top-tier legal professionals. What once required weeks of consultations and invoices totaling $15,000 can now begin with a single, well-crafted prompt. This is not about replacing lawyers entirely. It is about reclaiming control over the first, and often most expensive, layer of legal work: drafting. Whether it is a non-disclosure agreement, a freelance contract, or foundational LLC paperwork, the ability to generate structured, tailored, and context-aware documents has fundamentally changed the economics of building and protecting a business.

But access alone is not power. The real advantage lies in knowing how to ask. A vague prompt produces a vague contract. A precise, intentional prompt, however, can yield a document that is not only legally coherent but strategically aligned with your goals, capturing edge cases, defining boundaries, and protecting your interests with remarkable depth. This chapter is not just a collection of prompts. It is a framework for thinking like a high-level legal strategist, translating your needs into structured instructions that AI can execute with precision. Each prompt you are about to explore is designed to replace not just cost, but friction. To eliminate ambiguity. To accelerate decision-making. Because in this new landscape, the individuals who win will not be the ones with the biggest legal budgets. They will be the ones who know exactly what to ask for, and how to ask for it.

Framework 1
Skadden Arps NDA Architect

In today's information-driven economy, protecting confidential and proprietary information is critical to maintaining a competitive advantage. Whether it involves trade secrets, business strategies, client relationships, or proprietary technology, the unauthorized disclosure of sensitive information can result in significant financial and reputational damage. This is why Non-Disclosure Agreements (NDAs) are a foundational legal tool used by companies from startups to Fortune 500 enterprises, to safeguard their most valuable assets. A well-drafted NDA not only defines what information is protected, but also establishes clear obligations, limitations, and legal remedies, ensuring that all parties understand their responsibilities and the consequences of any breach. Many NDAs available online are overly generic and fail to address the specific nuances of a given business relationship. In high-stakes environments, such as corporate transactions, partnerships, or intellectual property discussions, these generic templates often leave critical gaps that can weaken enforceability. This prompt is designed to replicate the level of precision and comprehensiveness expected from a senior corporate attorney drafting agreements for large-scale, high-value engagements. By structuring the NDA across essential legal components, such as detailed definitions of confidential information, clearly defined exclusions, enforceable remedies, and jurisdictional clarity, the framework ensures that the agreement is both legally robust and practically enforceable. It also introduces optional provisions, such as non-solicitation clauses, allowing the agreement to be tailored to more complex business scenarios.

The result is a document that moves beyond boilerplate language and reflects a professional, institution-grade legal standard.

Non-Disclosure Agreement

You are a senior corporate attorney at Skadden Arps who drafts NDAs for Fortune 500 companies protecting trade secrets, client lists, and proprietary information worth billions, agreements that are airtight in court. I need a complete Non-Disclosure Agreement customized for my specific situation.

Draft:

1. Parties identification: clearly define who is disclosing and who is receiving confidential information
2. Definition of confidential information: specifically describe what is protected (trade secrets, business plans, financials, customer data, algorithms, formulas)
3. Mutual vs one-way: determine whether both parties share secrets (mutual NDA) or only one side discloses (one-way NDA)
4. Exclusions: standard carve-outs for information that becomes public, was already known, or is independently developed
5. Term and duration: how long the NDA lasts (typically 2-5 years) and whether obligations survive after termination
6. Permitted disclosures: when the receiving party CAN share information (court orders, regulatory requirements, employees who need to know)
7. Return or destruction clause: what happens to confidential materials when the relationship ends
8. Remedies for breach: injunctive relief, damages, and attorney's fees recoverable if someone violates the agreement
9. Non-solicitation addition: optionally prevent the other party from hiring your employees or poaching your clients
10. Governing law and jurisdiction: which state's law applies and where disputes must be resolved

Format as a complete, ready-to-sign NDA with standard legal formatting, signature blocks, and a plain-English summary of what each section means.

My NDA situation:

[DESCRIBE WHO YOU'RE SHARING INFORMATION WITH, WHAT TYPE OF INFORMATION IS BEING SHARED, AND WHETHER BOTH SIDES ARE SHARING OR JUST ONE]"

Q. How Users Can Apply This Prompt?

Users can apply this framework by clearly describing their specific NDA scenario, including who is involved, the nature of the information being shared, and whether the disclosure is one-way or mutual. This context allows the prompt to generate a customized agreement that aligns with the actual business relationship rather than relying on generic assumptions.

Once the details are provided, the prompt produces a complete, ready-to-sign NDA, structured with standard legal formatting, clearly defined clauses, and appropriate signature blocks. In addition to the formal agreement, the framework includes a plain-English summary of each section, helping users understand the purpose and implications of the legal language without requiring specialized legal knowledge. This dual approach ensures that the document is both legally sound and practically accessible, enabling users to confidently use it in real-world business situations.

Framework 2

The Wachtell Lipton Freelance and Contractor Agreement

Engaging independent contractors has become a standard practice for businesses seeking flexibility, specialized expertise, and cost efficiency. However, without a properly structured agreement, these relationships can expose both parties to significant legal and financial risks, ranging from worker misclassification issues and intellectual property disputes to scope creep and payment conflicts. A well-drafted independent contractor agreement serves as the foundation for a clear and enforceable working relationship, defining expectations, responsibilities, and protections on both sides. When executed correctly, it ensures that deliverables, ownership rights, and financial terms are aligned from the outset, reducing the likelihood of disputes and safeguarding long-term business interests.

Many freelance or contractor agreements rely on generic templates that fail to address critical legal nuances, particularly around independent contractor classification and intellectual property ownership. In professional legal environments, agreements are carefully structured to mitigate these risks by incorporating precise language that aligns with regulatory standards and protects against common points of conflict. This prompt is designed to replicate the level of rigor expected from top-tier corporate legal drafting, ensuring that all essential provisions, from work-for-hire clauses to liability limitations, are clearly defined and enforceable. By covering key elements such as scope clarity, payment structures, confidentiality, and termination rights, the framework minimizes ambiguity and prevents misunderstandings that often arise during engagements. It also balances protection for both parties, ensuring that the agreement is not only comprehensive but also fair and commercially practical.

The inclusion of structured clauses and legal safeguards helps create a document that can withstand scrutiny in real-world business and legal contexts.

The Freelance and Contractor Agreement

You are a senior associate at Wachtell Lipton who drafts independent contractor agreements that protect companies from misclassification lawsuits, scope creep disputes, and intellectual property ownership fights.

I need a complete freelance or independent contractor agreement that protects both parties.

Draft:

1. Scope of work: exactly what the contractor will deliver with specific milestones and deadlines
2. Payment terms: fixed project fee or hourly rate, payment schedule, invoicing process, and late payment penalties
3. Intellectual property assignment: all work product created during the engagement is owned by the hiring party
4. Work-for-hire clause: explicitly state that deliverables are "works made for hire" under copyright law
5. Independent contractor status: clear language establishing contractor is NOT an employee (critical for IRS compliance)
6. Confidentiality clause: contractor cannot share business secrets learned during the engagement
7. Non-compete scope: reasonable restrictions on contractor working with direct competitors during and after engagement
8. Revision and approval process: how many revision rounds are included and what triggers additional charges
9. Termination rights: how either party can end the agreement (with notice period) and what happens to partial work
10. Liability limitation: cap on damages and mutual indemnification so neither party faces unlimited financial exposure

Format as a complete, ready-to-sign independent contractor agreement with signature blocks and a plain-English summary of key terms.

My contractor situation:

[DESCRIBE WHETHER YOU'RE THE HIRING PARTY OR CONTRACTOR, THE TYPE OF WORK, PAYMENT STRUCTURE, AND TIMELINE]"

Q. How Users Can Apply This Prompt?

Users can apply this framework by providing a detailed description of their contractor arrangement, including whether they are the hiring party or the contractor, the nature of the work being performed, the agreed payment structure, and the expected timeline. This information allows the agreement to be tailored to the specific engagement rather than relying on generic assumptions.

Once the details are provided, the prompt generates a complete, ready-to-sign independent contractor agreement with standard legal formatting, clearly defined clauses, and signature blocks for both parties. In addition to the formal contract, the output includes a plain-English summary of key terms, enabling users to easily understand the practical implications of each provision. This approach ensures that the agreement is both legally robust and accessible, helping users establish a clear, professional, and well-protected working relationship from the outset.

Framework 3

The Sullivan & Cromwell LLC Operating Agreement

An LLC Operating Agreement is one of the most critical legal documents for any limited liability company, regardless of its size or complexity. It establishes the internal rules that govern how the business operates, how decisions are made, how profits are distributed, and how disputes are resolved. While some jurisdictions do not legally require an operating agreement, businesses that operate without one often face ambiguity around ownership rights, management authority, and financial arrangements, issues that can quickly escalate into costly disputes. A well-drafted agreement provides clarity, aligns expectations among members, and serves as a foundational framework that protects both the business and its owners over the long term. Many LLC operating agreements are created using generic templates that fail to reflect the unique structure and dynamics of a specific business. In professional legal practice, however, operating agreements are carefully tailored to address key variables such as ownership structure, capital contributions, governance models, and exit scenarios. This prompt is designed to replicate the level of precision and sophistication expected from top-tier corporate legal drafting, ensuring that the agreement is both comprehensive and adaptable to different business contexts, from single-member LLCs to multi-member partnerships. By covering essential provisions such as voting rights, transfer restrictions, profit allocation, and buyout mechanisms, the framework minimizes ambiguity and proactively addresses common areas of conflict. It also incorporates forward-looking elements, such as dissolution triggers and capital call provisions, which are often overlooked but critical in maintaining long-term stability.

The result is a document that is not only legally robust but also strategically structured to support the ongoing operation and evolution of the business.

Cromwell LLC Operating Agreement

You are a senior corporate attorney at Sullivan & Cromwell who structures LLC operating agreements for businesses ranging from solo freelancers to multi-member investment partnerships.

I need a complete LLC Operating Agreement that governs how my company runs, distributes profits, and handles disputes.

Structure:

1. Company formation: LLC name, state of formation, registered agent, and principal office address
2. Member information: names, ownership percentages, and initial capital contributions for each member
3. Management structure: member-managed (all owners vote) vs manager-managed (appointed leaders make decisions)
4. Capital contributions: what each member has invested (cash, property, services) and what happens if more capital is needed
5. Profit and loss allocation: how profits and losses are divided (pro rata by ownership or custom split)
6. Distribution schedule: when and how profits are distributed to members (monthly, quarterly, annually)
7. Voting rights: which decisions require majority vote vs unanimous consent (major decisions should require unanimous)
8. Transfer restrictions: can a member sell or transfer their ownership interest and does the LLC have right of first refusal
9. Dissolution triggers: what events cause the LLC to wind down (member death, bankruptcy, unanimous vote)
10. Buyout provisions: how a departing member's interest is valued and purchased by remaining members

Format as a complete LLC Operating Agreement with standard legal provisions, signature blocks, and a plain-English guide explaining each section.

My LLC:

[DESCRIBE YOUR BUSINESS, NUMBER OF MEMBERS, OWNERSHIP SPLIT, WHO MANAGES DAY-TO-DAY OPERATIONS, AND YOUR STATE OF FORMATION]"

Q. How Users Can Apply This Prompt?

Users can apply this framework by providing detailed information about their LLC structure, including the nature of the business, number of members, ownership percentages, management responsibilities, and the state in which the company is formed. These inputs allow the agreement to be customized to reflect the specific operational and legal requirements of the business.

Once the details are provided, the prompt generates a complete, ready-to-sign LLC Operating Agreement with standard legal formatting, clearly defined clauses, and signature blocks for all members. In addition, the output includes a plain-English guide explaining each section of the agreement, helping users understand the purpose and implications of the legal provisions without requiring specialized legal expertise. This dual-format approach ensures that the agreement is both legally enforceable and practically understandable, enabling business owners to establish a clear governance structure and operate with confidence.

Framework 4

The Kirkland & Ellis Service Agreement and Terms of Service

For any online business, whether a SaaS platform, mobile application, or digital product offering, Terms of Service (ToS) serve as the legal backbone that defines the relationship between the company and its users. These terms establish clear rules around how the service can be used, outline user responsibilities, and set boundaries that protect the business from misuse, disputes, and legal exposure. Without well-drafted Terms of Service, companies risk facing issues such as chargebacks, misuse of the platform, intellectual property conflicts, and costly litigation. A comprehensive ToS not only protects the business legally but also creates transparency and trust by clearly communicating what users can expect from the service.

Many businesses rely on generic or copy-pasted Terms of Service that fail to address the specific risks associated with their product, pricing model, or user behavior. In professional legal practice, Terms of Service are carefully structured to anticipate real-world scenarios, such as payment disputes, platform misuse, or liability claims, and to mitigate those risks through precise and enforceable language. This prompt is designed to replicate the level of rigor expected from top-tier technology legal drafting, ensuring that all critical provisions are covered in a structured and legally sound manner. By incorporating key elements such as limitation of liability, acceptable use policies, dispute resolution mechanisms, and intellectual property protections, the framework ensures that the agreement is both comprehensive and defensible. It also balances legal protection with usability by including a plain-English summary, making the terms accessible to users while maintaining their legal integrity. The result is a document that not only safeguards the business but also aligns with best practices followed by leading SaaS and digital platforms.

Kirkland & Ellis Service Agreement and Terms of Service

You are a senior technology attorney at Kirkland & Ellis who drafts Terms of Service and Service Agreements for SaaS companies, digital product sellers, and online service providers, protecting them from lawsuits, chargebacks, and unreasonable customer demands.

I need complete Terms of Service for my website, app, or online business.

Draft:

1. Service description: what the user gets, what the platform does, and what it explicitly does NOT promise
2. Account responsibilities: users must provide accurate information, maintain password security, and accept responsibility for all activity under their account
3. Payment and billing terms: pricing, billing cycles, auto-renewal, refund policy, and what happens if payment fails
4. Acceptable use policy: prohibited behaviors (spam, harassment, illegal activity, reverse engineering) with enforcement rights
5. Intellectual property: the company owns all platform content and the user owns their uploaded content (with a license grant for platform use)
6. Limitation of liability: cap liability at the amount paid in the last 12 months (never unlimited exposure)
7. Disclaimer of warranties: services provided "as is" without guarantees of uptime, accuracy, or fitness for a particular purpose
8. Termination rights: the company can suspend or terminate accounts that violate terms with or without notice
9. Dispute resolution: mandatory arbitration clause vs litigation, class action waiver, and governing law
10. Privacy policy reference: link to the separate privacy policy and user consent to data practices

Format as complete, ready-to-publish Terms of Service with standard legal formatting and a plain-English FAQ summary users can actually understand.

My business:

[DESCRIBE YOUR PRODUCT OR SERVICE]

Q. How Users Can Apply This Prompt?

Users can apply this framework by providing details about their business model, including the type of product or service offered, whether it operates as a website, app, or SaaS platform, the pricing structure, and whether user data is collected. This information allows the Terms of Service to be tailored to the specific operational and legal requirements of the business.

Once the inputs are provided, the prompt generates a complete, ready-to-publish Terms of Service document with standard legal formatting and clearly defined clauses covering all essential areas. In addition, it includes a plain-English FAQ-style summary that explains key provisions in a user-friendly manner, helping customers understand their rights and obligations without needing legal expertise. This approach ensures that the final output is both legally robust and practically effective, enabling businesses to operate with confidence while minimizing legal risk.

Framework 5

The Latham & Watkins Privacy Policy Generator

In an increasingly data-driven digital environment, the way businesses collect, use, and protect personal information is subject to intense regulatory scrutiny. Laws such as the General Data Protection Regulation (GDPR) and the California Consumer Privacy Act (CCPA) have established strict requirements for transparency, user consent, and data protection, with significant financial penalties for non-compliance. A well-drafted privacy policy is not merely a legal formality, it is a critical document that informs users about how their data is handled, establishes trust, and ensures that a business operates within the boundaries of global data protection standards. For any website, application, or online service, a comprehensive privacy policy is essential to mitigate legal risk and demonstrate responsible data stewardship.

Many privacy policies available online are generic, outdated, or fail to meet the specific requirements of modern data protection laws. In professional legal practice, privacy policies are carefully structured to reflect the actual data practices of a business, ensuring alignment with regulatory obligations across jurisdictions. This prompt is designed to replicate the rigor expected from top-tier data privacy legal drafting, incorporating key elements required for compliance with GDPR, CCPA, and other global standards. By explicitly addressing areas such as data collection methods, user rights, third-party data sharing, and retention policies, the framework ensures that the resulting document is both legally comprehensive and operationally accurate. It also emphasizes transparency and clarity, which are central to regulatory compliance and user trust. The inclusion of a plain-English summary further enhances accessibility, making the policy understandable to users while maintaining its legal effectiveness.

The Privacy Policy Generator

You are a senior data privacy attorney at Latham & Watkins who drafts privacy policies compliant with GDPR, CCPA, and global data protection regulations, because a non-compliant privacy policy can trigger fines of $7,500 per violation under CCPA and €20 million under GDPR.

I need a complete privacy policy for my website or application.

Draft:

1. Information collected: exactly what personal data I collect (names, emails, phone numbers, IP addresses, cookies, payment information)
2. Collection methods: how I collect data (forms, cookies, analytics, third-party integrations, automatic collection)
3. Purpose of collection: why I collect each type of data (account creation, payment processing, marketing, analytics)
4. Data sharing: which third parties receive user data (payment processors, email services, analytics tools, advertising)
5. Cookie policy: what cookies I use, what they track, and how users can opt out
6. User rights: right to access, correct, delete, and export personal data (required by GDPR and CCPA)
7. Data retention: how long I keep each type of data and when it's permanently deleted
8. Security measures: how I protect personal data (encryption, access controls, secure servers)
9. Children's privacy: compliance with COPPA if any users might be under 13
10. Contact information: how users can reach my data protection officer or privacy contact with questions or requests

Format as a complete, legally compliant privacy policy covering GDPR, CCPA, and general best practices with a plain-English summary at the top.

My data practices:

[DESCRIBE YOUR WEBSITE OR APP, WHAT USER DATA YOU COLLECT, WHICH THIRD-PARTY SERVICES YOU USE, AND WHERE YOUR USERS ARE LOCATED]

Q. How Users Can Apply This Prompt?

Users can apply this framework by providing a detailed description of their data practices, including the type of platform they operate (website or application), the categories of personal data they collect, the tools and third-party services they use, and the geographic location of their users. These inputs allow the privacy policy to be tailored to the specific regulatory requirements and operational realities of the business.

Once the information is provided, the prompt generates a complete, ready-to-publish privacy policy that addresses all critical aspects of data protection, from collection and usage to security and user rights. In addition, it includes a plain-English summary at the beginning, helping users quickly understand how their data is handled. This approach ensures that the final document is both legally compliant and user-friendly, enabling businesses to operate confidently while meeting global data protection obligations.

Framework 6

The Davis Polk Employment Offer Letter

An employment offer letter or agreement is more than just a formal invitation to join a company, it is a critical legal document that defines the terms of the working relationship from day one. It establishes expectations around compensation, responsibilities, confidentiality, and ownership of work, while also protecting the company from potential disputes related to termination, intellectual property, and competitive activity. In today's dynamic employment landscape, where remote work, equity compensation, and knowledge-based roles are increasingly common, a well-structured agreement is essential to ensure clarity, alignment, and legal protection for both the employer and the employee. Many employment agreements rely on generic templates that fail to address key legal and operational risks, particularly in areas such as intellectual property ownership, non-compete enforceability, and at-will employment clarity. In professional legal practice, these agreements are carefully drafted to balance compliance with employment laws while safeguarding the company's interests. This prompt is designed to replicate the level of rigor and precision expected from top-tier employment law drafting, ensuring that all essential provisions are clearly defined and enforceable.

By incorporating structured clauses covering compensation, equity, confidentiality, and post-employment restrictions, the framework minimizes ambiguity and reduces the likelihood of future disputes. It also accounts for jurisdiction-specific considerations, such as the enforceability of non-compete clauses, making the agreement both practical and legally sound. The result is a document that not only formalizes the employment relationship but also provides comprehensive protection and clarity for both parties.

Davis Polk Employment Offer Letter

You are a senior employment attorney at Davis Polk who drafts offer letters and employment agreements that protect companies from wrongful termination suits, non-compete disputes, and intellectual property theft by departing employees.

I need a complete employment offer letter or agreement.

Draft:

1. Position details: job title, reporting structure, start date, work location (on-site, remote, hybrid)
2. Compensation: base salary, payment frequency, and eligibility for bonuses or commission with structure
3. Equity or stock options: if applicable, number of shares, vesting schedule, strike price, and cliff period
4. Benefits summary: health insurance, dental, vision, 401K match, PTO days, and any unique perks
5. At-will employment: clear statement that either party can end the relationship at any time with or without cause
6. Confidentiality obligations: employee agrees not to disclose trade secrets during and after employment
7. Intellectual property assignment: everything created during employment using company resources belongs to the company
8. Non-compete clause: reasonable restrictions on working for competitors after leaving (state-specific enforceability)
9. Non-solicitation clause: cannot recruit company employees or solicit company clients for a defined period after departure
10. Severance terms: what the employee receives if terminated without cause (if applicable)

Format as a complete employment offer letter with standard legal provisions, acceptance signature block, and a plain-English summary.

My hiring situation:

[DESCRIBE THE ROLE, COMPENSATION PACKAGE, WHETHER EQUITY IS INVOLVED, YOUR STATE, AND ANY SPECIFIC RESTRICTIONS YOU WANT]

Q. How Users Can Apply This Prompt?

Users can apply this framework by providing detailed information about their hiring situation, including the role being offered, compensation structure, any equity or stock options involved, the applicable state or jurisdiction, and any specific restrictions or requirements they wish to include. These inputs allow the agreement to be tailored to the specific needs of the company and the position. Once the details are provided, the prompt generates a complete, ready-to-sign employment offer letter or agreement with standard legal formatting, clearly defined terms, and an acceptance signature block.

In addition, it includes a plain-English summary of key provisions, enabling both parties to understand the agreement without requiring specialized legal knowledge. This approach ensures that the final document is both legally robust and accessible, helping establish a clear, professional, and well-protected employment relationship from the outset.

Framework 7

The Cravath Swaine Partnership and Co-Founder Agreement

A co-founder relationship is one of the most critical and potentially fragile elements of any startup. While early-stage ventures often focus on product development and market traction, many overlook the importance of clearly defining how founders will work together, make decisions, and handle conflict. In reality, a significant number of startups fail not because of market conditions, but due to internal disagreements, misaligned expectations, and unclear ownership structures. A well-drafted co-founder agreement serves as the foundation for alignment, establishing clear rules around equity, roles, decision-making, and exit scenarios. It ensures that all founders are aligned not only on the vision, but also on the practical realities of building and scaling a business together. Many founding teams delay formalizing their agreement or rely on informal understandings, which can lead to serious conflicts as the business grows. In professional legal practice, co-founder agreements are structured with precision and foresight, anticipating potential areas of dispute such as equity ownership, vesting, control rights, and founder departures. This prompt is designed to replicate the rigor expected from top-tier startup legal drafting, ensuring that the agreement addresses both current expectations and future contingencies.

By incorporating critical provisions such as vesting schedules, intellectual property assignment, decision-making frameworks, and deadlock resolution mechanisms, the framework proactively mitigates the most common sources of founder conflict. It also balances fairness with protection, ensuring that contributions are recognized while preventing scenarios where one founder benefits disproportionately without long-term commitment. The result is a document that is not only comprehensive but also strategically designed to preserve founder alignment and business continuity.

Partnership and Co-Founder Agreement

You are a senior partnership attorney at Cravath Swaine who drafts co-founder agreements for startups, the single most important legal document for any business with more than one founder, because 65% of startups fail due to co-founder disputes.

I need a complete co-founder agreement that prevents the fights that kill startups.

Draft:

1. Equity split: percentage ownership for each founder with clear justification for the split
2. Vesting schedule: 4-year vesting with 1-year cliff so no founder walks away with free equity after 2 months
3. Role definition: who is CEO, CTO, COO, clear responsibilities to prevent stepping on each other's toes
4. Decision-making authority: which decisions each founder can make alone vs which require agreement from all founders
5. Salary and compensation: when founders start paying themselves and how much relative to the business stage
6. IP assignment: all intellectual property created for the business belongs to the company, not individual founders
7. Full-time commitment: founders must work full-time on the business and cannot run competing side projects
8. Deadlock resolution: what happens when founders disagree on a critical decision and can't reach consensus
9. Exit provisions: how a departing founder's equity is handled (buyback at fair market value, vesting acceleration or forfeiture)
10. Drag-along and tag-along rights: if one founder wants to sell, the other can force or join the sale under certain conditions

Format as a complete co-founder agreement with vesting schedule, decision matrix, and exit provisions ready for attorney review.

Our startup:

[DESCRIBE YOUR BUSINESS, NUMBER OF CO-FOUNDERS, PROPOSED EQUITY SPLIT, ROLES, AND ANY EXISTING DISAGREEMENTS ABOUT STRUCTURE]

Q. How Users Can Apply This Prompt?

Users can apply this framework by providing detailed information about their startup structure, including the number of co-founders, proposed equity split, individual roles, and any existing areas of disagreement or uncertainty. These inputs allow the agreement to be tailored to the specific dynamics of the founding team rather than relying on generic assumptions. Once the details are provided, the prompt generates a complete co-founder agreement with structured provisions covering equity, vesting, governance, and exit scenarios. It includes elements such as a vesting schedule, decision-making matrix, and clearly defined exit provisions, all formatted in a way that is ready for professional legal review. This ensures that the agreement is both practically useful and legally robust, giving founders a clear framework to operate within and significantly reducing the risk of disputes that could derail the business.

Framework 8

The Gibson Dunn Cease and Desist Letter

When intellectual property or legal rights are infringed, swift and decisive action is essential to prevent further harm and protect what you have built. A cease and desist letter is often the first and most effective step in enforcing those rights, allowing the issue to be addressed without immediately resorting to costly and time-consuming litigation. When drafted properly, such a letter communicates the seriousness of the matter, outlines the legal basis for the claim, and provides the recipient with a clear opportunity to correct their actions. In many cases, a well-structured and professionally worded letter is sufficient to secure compliance, preserving both time and resources while maintaining a strong legal position. Generic cease and desist templates often lack the specificity and authority required to compel action, making them easier for recipients to ignore or challenge. In professional legal practice, these letters are carefully crafted to combine clear factual evidence, strong legal grounding, and a firm but measured tone. This prompt is designed to replicate the approach taken by top-tier litigation counsel, ensuring that every element, from the identification of rights to the articulation of legal consequences is presented with precision and credibility.

By requiring detailed descriptions of the infringement, supporting evidence, and explicit legal references, the framework strengthens the enforceability of the claim and signals that the sender is prepared to escalate the matter if necessary. At the same time, it maintains a professional tone that avoids unnecessary hostility while still conveying urgency and seriousness. The result is a document that is both persuasive and strategically effective, increasing the likelihood of compliance without immediate legal escalation.

Gibson Dunn Cease and Desist Letter

You are a senior litigation partner at Gibson Dunn who writes cease and desist letters so professionally intimidating that 90% of recipients comply without the matter ever reaching court — saving clients $50,000+ in litigation costs.

I need a cease and desist letter that stops someone from infringing on my rights.

Draft:

1. Identification of rights: clearly state what I own (trademark, copyright, patent, trade secret, contractual right) with registration numbers if applicable
2. Description of infringement: specifically describe exactly what the other party is doing that violates my rights
3. Evidence documentation: reference specific instances with dates, screenshots, URLs, or other proof of infringement
4. Legal basis: cite the specific laws being violated (Lanham Act for trademark, DMCA for copyright, state contract law)
5. Demand to cease: explicitly demand they stop all infringing activity by a specific deadline (typically 10-15 business days)
6. Demand to desist: require they never resume the infringing behavior in the future
7. Remedial actions: demand removal of infringing content, destruction of materials, or public correction
8. Damages reserved: state that I reserve the right to pursue all legal remedies including monetary damages
9. Consequences of non-compliance: clearly state that legal action will follow if demands are not met by the deadline
10. Professional but firm tone: authoritative language that signals I have counsel and will act, without being threatening or abusive

Format as a complete cease and desist letter ready to send with professional legal formatting and firm tone.

My situation:

[DESCRIBE WHAT SOMEONE IS DOING THAT VIOLATES YOUR RIGHTS, WHAT RIGHTS THEY'RE INFRINGING, AND WHAT OUTCOME YOU WANT]

Q. How Users Can Apply This Prompt?

Users can apply this framework by clearly describing their specific situation, including the nature of the rights being infringed, the actions taken by the other party, and the outcome they are seeking. Providing details such as dates, examples of infringement, and any available evidence allows the letter to be tailored with accuracy and authority. Once the information is provided, the prompt generates a complete, ready-to-send cease and desist letter with professional legal formatting and a firm, authoritative tone. It includes clearly defined demands, a reasonable compliance deadline, and a statement of reserved legal rights, ensuring that the recipient understands both the issue and the potential consequences of non-compliance. This approach enables users to take immediate, effective action to protect their rights while maintaining a strong legal and professional stance.

Framework 9

The Cleary Gottlieb Demand Letter for Payment

Unpaid invoices and overdue payments can significantly impact cash flow, strain business operations, and create unnecessary financial uncertainty. While legal action is always an option, it is often time-consuming, expensive, and disruptive. In many cases, a professionally drafted demand letter serves as the most effective first step in recovering what is owed clearly outlining the obligation, documenting prior attempts to resolve the issue, and signaling a readiness to escalate if necessary. When executed properly, a demand letter not only reinforces the seriousness of the claim but also provides the debtor with a final opportunity to resolve the matter quickly and avoid formal litigation.

Many informal payment requests fail because they lack structure, legal grounding, or the authority required to prompt action. In professional legal practice, demand letters are carefully crafted to combine clear documentation, precise legal claims, and firm deadlines, creating both pressure and clarity for the recipient. This prompt is designed to replicate the approach used by experienced commercial litigation attorneys, ensuring that the letter is not only persuasive but also legally grounded and strategically effective. By incorporating elements such as a detailed breakdown of the amount owed, a documented history of collection efforts, and a clearly stated legal basis, the framework strengthens the credibility of the claim. It also introduces practical components such as specific payment instructions and optional settlement incentives, that increase the likelihood of prompt resolution. The result is a letter that moves beyond a simple request and becomes a formal, actionable demand for payment.

Cleary Gottlieb Demand Letter for Payment

You are a senior commercial litigation attorney at Cleary Gottlieb who writes demand letters that recover unpaid invoices, overdue payments, and breached contract amounts, getting clients their money without filing a lawsuit.

I need a demand letter that gets someone to pay what they owe me.

Draft:

1. Debtor identification: full legal name and address of the person or company who owes the money
2. Debt documentation: reference the specific contract, invoice, agreement, or verbal promise that created the obligation
3. Amount owed: the exact total including the original amount, accrued interest, late fees, and any penalties
4. Payment history: note any partial payments made and the remaining balance
5. Timeline of attempts: document previous invoices sent, emails exchanged, and calls made to collect
6. Legal basis: breach of contract, unjust enrichment, or account stated, the specific legal claim
7. Payment deadline: demand full payment within 10-15 business days of receiving the letter
8. Payment method: specify exactly how to pay (wire transfer, check, ACH) with account details or mailing address
9. Consequences: if payment isn't received, I will pursue legal action including filing a lawsuit and seeking attorney's fees
10. Settlement offer: optionally offer a small discount for immediate payment to incentivize quick resolution

Format as a complete demand letter ready to send with professional legal formatting, firm tone, and certified mail instructions.

My situation:

[DESCRIBE WHO OWES YOU MONEY, THE AMOUNT, WHAT THE PAYMENT WAS FOR, AND WHAT COLLECTION EFFORTS YOU'VE ALREADY MADE]

Q. How Users Can Apply This Prompt?

Users can apply this framework by providing a detailed description of their specific situation, including who owes the money, the total amount due, the underlying agreement or transaction, and any prior attempts made to collect payment. The more precise the information, the stronger and more effective the resulting letter will be. Once these details are provided, the prompt generates a complete, ready-to-send demand letter with professional legal formatting, a firm and authoritative tone, and clear instructions for payment. It includes a defined deadline, outlines the consequences of non-compliance, and may incorporate a settlement option to encourage quick resolution. This approach enables users to take structured and effective action to recover outstanding payments, often resolving the matter without the need for costly legal proceedings.

Framework 10

The Fenwick & West Intellectual Property Protection Suit

In today's competitive and innovation-driven landscape, a company's most valuable assets are often intangible, its brand, technology, proprietary processes, and creative output. Without a structured approach to protecting these assets, businesses risk losing control over their intellectual property, facing infringement issues, or missing opportunities to secure long-term competitive advantage. A comprehensive intellectual property (IP) protection plan ensures that these assets are properly identified, legally protected, and strategically managed. By combining legal safeguards such as trademarks, copyrights, patents, and trade secrets with proactive enforcement and monitoring, businesses can preserve their value, strengthen their market position, and mitigate legal risk.

Many businesses take a fragmented approach to intellectual property, addressing issues reactively rather than proactively. In professional legal practice, however, IP protection is treated as a holistic strategy, where each form of protection trademark, copyright, patent, and trade secret is evaluated in the context of the overall business model. This prompt is designed to replicate the level of rigor and strategic thinking applied by top-tier technology and intellectual property law firms, ensuring that no critical area is overlooked. By systematically addressing trademark availability, registration processes, copyright ownership, trade secret protection, and patent eligibility, the framework provides a comprehensive roadmap for securing and maintaining IP rights. It also extends beyond registration to include enforcement protocols, contractual protections, and ongoing audits, ensuring that the strategy remains effective as the business evolves. The result is not just a checklist, but a structured, long-term IP protection system aligned with industry best practices.

Fenwick & West Intellectual Property Protection Suit

You are a senior intellectual property attorney at Fenwick & West, the Silicon Valley law firm that has protected the IP of Google, Apple, and Facebook, who builds complete IP protection strategies for businesses.

I need a complete intellectual property protection plan for my business.

Protect:

1. Trademark assessment: is my business name, logo, or slogan trademarkable and is anyone already using something similar
2. Trademark search strategy: how to search the USPTO database and common law sources for potential conflicts
3. Trademark application guide: the exact steps, classifications, and specimens needed to file a federal trademark
4. Copyright protection: what content I create that's automatically copyrighted and when to register for additional protection
5. Trade secret identification: what proprietary information I have (processes, formulas, client lists) and how to legally protect it
6. Patent assessment: do I have any inventions or unique processes that qualify for patent protection
7. Domain name protection: secure my brand across .com, .net, .io, and social media handles before someone else does
8. Employee and contractor IP clauses: provisions that ensure everything created for my business belongs to my business
9. Cease and desist protocol: what to do when someone infringes my IP and the escalation steps from letter to lawsuit
10. Annual IP audit checklist: a yearly review to ensure all protections are current and no new vulnerabilities have emerged

Format as a Fenwick & West-style IP protection plan with an asset inventory, registration guide, and annual maintenance checklist.

My business:

[DESCRIBE YOUR BUSINESS NAME, PRODUCTS, ANY LOGOS OR SLOGANS, PROPRIETARY PROCESSES, AND EXISTING IP REGISTRATIONS IF ANY]

Q. How Users Can Apply This Prompt?

Users can apply this framework by providing detailed information about their business and intellectual property assets, including their business name, logos, slogans, products or services, proprietary processes, and any existing registrations. This information allows the plan to be tailored to the specific nature and needs of the business. Once the details are provided, the prompt generates a complete IP protection plan that includes an asset inventory, step-by-step registration guidance, and an annual maintenance checklist. It outlines how to secure trademarks, protect creative works, safeguard trade secrets, and evaluate patent opportunities, while also providing practical steps for enforcement and risk mitigation. This approach ensures that users not only understand what protections are available but also how to implement and maintain them effectively, resulting in a professional, strategic framework for managing intellectual property over time.

The AI Financial Shield: Build Dalio-Level Protection for Your Money

Claude can now protect your money from banks, inflation, and even systemic shocks, just like the strategies used inside Ray Dalio's $150B hedge fund… and you can do it for free.

This isn't theory. This isn't hype.
This is a shift in how personal finance works.

For the first time, anyone can use AI to think like a hedge fund, analyzing risks, diversifying intelligently, and building systems designed to survive uncertainty. The kind of financial protection that was once reserved for billion-dollar institutions is now accessible through something as simple as the right prompts.

Markets are unpredictable. Inflation erodes silently. And traditional banking systems don't always work in your favor. But with AI, you can start building a system that adapts, protects, and evolves just like the strategies Ray Dalio has been advocating for years. In this chapter, you'll discover six powerful Claude prompts that go beyond basic budgeting or investing. These are designed to help you build your own financial defense system, one that is resilient, intelligent, and aligned with the realities of today's world.

This is not just about managing money.
It's about protecting it. Growing it. And taking control of it.

Framework 1

Financial Dependency Risk Audit Framework

In an increasingly digital financial ecosystem, individuals and businesses rely heavily on banks and payment processors to store, move, and manage their money. While these systems provide convenience and accessibility, they also introduce hidden costs, operational constraints, and centralized points of control that are often overlooked. Fees that appear insignificant on a monthly basis can accumulate into meaningful annual expenses, while restrictions such as withdrawal limits, transfer delays, or sudden account freezes can disrupt liquidity at critical moments. Conducting a structured audit of these dependencies is essential to gaining full visibility into how financial infrastructure impacts both cost efficiency and operational resilience. Most people evaluate their financial setup at a surface level, focusing on balances, transactions, or basic fees—without fully understanding the systemic dependencies and risks embedded within their banking relationships. In professional financial analysis, however, these factors are examined holistically, with particular attention to cost accumulation, control mechanisms, and failure scenarios. This prompt is designed to replicate that level of rigor by systematically uncovering every fee, restriction, and single point of failure across a user's financial ecosystem.

By converting all costs into annual figures, the framework reveals the true financial impact of banking relationships. At the same time, it identifies operational risks such as account freezes or reliance on a single provider, that could materially affect access to funds. The inclusion of a quantified dependency score and a prioritized action list ensures that the analysis moves beyond observation and becomes a decision-making tool focused on risk reduction and financial optimization.

Auditing your Bank Dependency

ROLE:

Act as a financial independence analyst who identifies every hidden way banks and payment processors control your money and charge you for the privilege.

TASK:

Audit my complete financial setup and show every fee, restriction, and dependency I have on banks and payment processors.

STEPS:

1. Ask for my current banks, payment processors, and monthly transaction volume before starting
2. Calculate total annual fees paid to banks and processors
3. Identify every restriction, withdrawal limits, account freezes, transfer delays
4. Map every single point of failure, what happens if one account gets shut down
5. Deliver a dependency score and a priority list of what to fix first

RULES:

1. Every fee must be calculated annually, monthly fees feel small, annual fees feel real
2. Single points of failure must be flagged as critical risks
3. Dependency score must be specific, not just "high" or "low"
4. Priority list ordered by financial risk, not ease of fixing

OUTPUT:

Annual Fee Total → Restriction Map → Single Points of Failure → Dependency Score → Priority Fix List

Q. How Users Can Apply This Prompt?

Users can apply this framework by providing a detailed overview of their current financial setup, including the banks they use, payment processors they rely on, and their approximate monthly transaction volume. These inputs allow the analysis to map out the full structure of their financial dependencies. Once the information is provided, the prompt evaluates the total annual cost of maintaining these relationships, identifies all relevant restrictions and limitations, and highlights any single points of failure that could disrupt access to funds. It then assigns a clear dependency score and produces a prioritized list of actions to reduce risk and improve efficiency.

The final output delivers a comprehensive, structured view of financial dependency, enabling users to make more informed decisions about where to consolidate, diversify, or restructure their financial infrastructur

Framework 2

Financial Resilience & Income Independence Framework

In a world where financial systems are increasingly centralized and digitally controlled, the ability to maintain uninterrupted income flow has become a critical component of financial resilience. Solopreneurs and independent operators, in particular, are often heavily reliant on a limited number of banks or payment processors, creating vulnerabilities that can disrupt revenue overnight. Account freezes, processor shutdowns, regulatory changes, or cross-border payment restrictions can all impact access to funds, regardless of how strong the underlying business may be. Building an income system that is diversified, flexible, and resistant to single points of failure is no longer optional, it is a strategic necessity for long-term financial stability.

Most income systems are designed for convenience rather than resilience, prioritizing simplicity over robustness. As a result, many individuals unknowingly create critical dependencies on a single payment rail, platform, or jurisdiction, exposing themselves to avoidable risk. In professional financial planning, however, income infrastructure is treated as a system that must withstand disruption, not just operate efficiently under normal conditions. This prompt is designed to replicate that level of strategic thinking by identifying potential disruption scenarios and proactively designing around them. It enforces key principles such as multi-channel payment architecture, geographic diversification, and rapid-response contingency planning, ensuring that income can continue to flow even if one or more components fail. By focusing on practical, currently available tools and legally compliant structures, the framework delivers a solution that is both actionable and resilient.

Bank-Independent Revenue System Design

ROLE: Act as a financial freedom architect who builds income systems for solopreneurs that work even when banks freeze accounts, payment processors shut down, or governments restrict transactions.

TASK: Design a complete income system that keeps money flowing no matter what any single bank, processor, or government decides to do.

STEPS:

1. Ask for my income sources, countries I work with, and current payment setup before starting
2. Identify the three most likely ways my income could be disrupted
3. Build a multi-channel payment system, never dependent on one processor
4. Design a geographic diversification plan, income received across multiple jurisdictions
5. Create a 30-day emergency protocol, exactly what to do if my main account gets frozen

RULES:

1. System must function if any single payment processor shuts down
2. Emergency protocol must be executable in under 24 hours
3. Geographic diversification must be legal and specific, not theoretical
4. Every recommended tool must be available to solopreneurs right now

OUTPUT:

Disruption Risk Map → Multi-Channel Payment System → Geographic Plan → 30-Day Emergency Protocol

Q. How Users Can Apply This Prompt?

Users can apply this framework by providing a clear overview of their current income structure, including revenue sources, the countries they operate in, and the payment systems they rely on. These inputs allow the analysis to identify specific vulnerabilities and tailor the system accordingly.

Once the information is provided, the prompt maps out the most likely disruption risks and designs a multi-channel payment system that eliminates reliance on any single processor. It also outlines a geographic diversification strategy, ensuring that income streams are distributed across multiple jurisdictions in a compliant and practical manner. Finally, it delivers a 30-day emergency protocol a clear, step-by-step plan that can be executed quickly if access to primary financial channels is disrupted. The result is a robust, future-proof income infrastructure that prioritizes continuity, control, and adaptability, enabling users to operate with greater confidence in an uncertain financial environment.

Framework 3

Payment Cost Optimization & Elimination Framework

In modern digital commerce, payment infrastructure plays a critical role in enabling revenue, but it also introduces significant and often underestimated costs. Transaction fees, currency conversion charges, wire transfer costs, and chargeback losses can quietly erode margins, particularly for businesses operating across borders. While these costs are typically accepted as a standard cost of doing business, advances in alternative payment rails, such as Bitcoin and stablecoins have created new opportunities to optimize or even eliminate certain categories of fees. A structured approach to analyzing and redesigning payment flows can unlock meaningful savings while improving overall financial efficiency.

Most businesses lack full visibility into the true cost of their payment systems, as fees are fragmented across multiple providers and often embedded within transactions. In professional financial optimization, these costs are aggregated, analyzed, and strategically reduced through targeted infrastructure changes rather than broad assumptions. This prompt is designed to replicate that analytical rigor by calculating total annual payment costs including hidden expenses and identifying where alternative payment methods can be applied effectively.

By distinguishing between use cases suited for Bitcoin (where decentralization and lower fees may be advantageous) and stablecoins (where price stability is essential), the framework ensures that recommendations are both practical and context-specific. The phased migration approach further reduces operational risk, allowing users to transition gradually while maintaining business continuity. The result is a data-driven cost optimization strategy rather than a theoretical exercise.

Zero-Fee Payment Infrastructure Strategy

ROLE: Act as a payment optimization specialist who eliminates unnecessary transaction fees using Bitcoin, stablecoins, and direct payment rails.

TASK: Calculate exactly what I pay in payment fees annually and build a plan to eliminate as much of it as possible.

STEPS:

1. Ask for my annual revenue, payment processors used, and countries I invoice before starting
2. Calculate total annual fees: processing, currency conversion, wire transfers, chargebacks
3. Identify which transactions are best suited for Bitcoin payments
4. Identify which transactions are best suited for stablecoin payments
5. Build a migration plan, move highest-fee transactions first
6. Calculate projected annual savings after migration

RULES:

1. Fee calculation must include hidden costs: chargebacks, currency conversion, withdrawal fees
2. Migration plan must be phased, never move everything at once
3. Bitcoin recommendation only for clients comfortable with volatility
4. Stablecoin recommendation for clients who need price stability
5. End with: "This is not financial advice"

OUTPUT:

Annual Fee Calculation → Bitcoin Opportunities → Stablecoin Opportunities → Migration Plan → Projected Savings

Q. How Users Can Apply This Prompt?

Users can apply this framework by providing key details about their financial operations, including annual revenue, payment processors used, and the countries in which they invoice clients. These inputs enable a comprehensive assessment of current payment costs and transaction patterns.

Once the information is provided, the prompt calculates the total annual fees across all payment channels, identifies high-cost transactions, and evaluates where alternative payment methods can be introduced. It then outlines a phased migration plan, prioritizing the highest-impact opportunities first, while ensuring that the transition remains operationally manageable. Finally, it delivers a projection of potential annual savings, giving users a clear view of the financial impact. The outcome is a structured, actionable plan to reduce payment-related expenses, improve margin efficiency, and build a more cost-effective payment infrastructure. This is not financial advice.

Framework 4

Inflation Protection & Purchasing Power Preservation Framework

Inflation is one of the most persistent and often underestimated forces affecting personal wealth. While nominal balances may appear stable or even growing, the real value of money, what it can actually purchase can steadily decline over time. In environments where interest rates on savings accounts remain low and monetary expansion continues, holding large amounts of idle cash can result in a silent erosion of purchasing power. Protecting against this requires a deliberate and structured approach to asset allocation, one that not only preserves value but positions capital to grow in real terms over the long term.

Many individuals underestimate the true impact of inflation because it is rarely presented in tangible terms. Percentage figures often fail to convey how much actual purchasing power is lost year over year. In professional wealth management, however, inflation is addressed through real-return-focused strategies, where capital is allocated across assets designed to outpace currency devaluation. This prompt is designed to replicate that level of rigor by translating inflation into real monetary impact, identifying vulnerable areas of a portfolio, and constructing a structured plan to mitigate those risks. By combining risk-aligned asset allocation with a disciplined rebalancing strategy, the framework ensures that the approach remains both practical and sustainable over time. The inclusion of a long-term comparison further reinforces the importance of proactive action, illustrating the compounding effect of inflation versus the benefits of strategic allocation. This transforms inflation protection from a conceptual concern into a quantifiable and actionable strategy.

The Inflation-Resilient Wealth Framework

ROLE: Act as an inflation protection strategist who builds asset allocation plans that preserve purchasing power when governments print money and banks pay 0.01% interest.

TASK: Build a complete inflation protection plan that keeps my money growing faster than the government can devalue it.

STEPS:

1. Ask for my current savings, monthly income, and risk tolerance before starting
2. Calculate how much purchasing power I've already lost to inflation this year
3. Identify the highest-risk savings, cash sitting in low-interest accounts
4. Build an allocation plan across inflation-resistant assets
5. Design a monthly rebalancing schedule that runs automatically
6. Show the 10-year difference between doing nothing and implementing the plan

RULES:

1. Purchasing power loss must be calculated in real dollar terms, not percentages
2. Allocation plan must match my risk tolerance, never aggressive by default
3. Rebalancing schedule must be specific, exact date and exact action per month
4. 10-year comparison must use conservative assumptions
5. End with: "This is not financial advice"

OUTPUT:

Purchasing Power Loss → High-Risk Savings Identified → Allocation Plan → Monthly Schedule → 10-Year Comparison

Q. How Users Can Apply This Prompt?

Users can apply this framework by providing key financial inputs, including their current savings, monthly income, and risk tolerance. These details establish the foundation for a personalized analysis that reflects both financial capacity and comfort with risk.

Once the information is provided, the prompt calculates the real purchasing power lost to inflation, identifies portions of capital that are most exposed such as cash held in low-yield accounts and develops a tailored allocation plan across inflation-resistant assets. It also outlines a specific monthly rebalancing schedule, ensuring that the strategy is maintained consistently without requiring constant oversight. Finally, it presents a 10-year comparison, demonstrating the projected difference between maintaining the current approach and implementing the proposed plan. The result is a structured, forward-looking framework that helps preserve and grow real wealth over time, enabling users to make informed decisions in the face of ongoing inflationary pressures. This is not financial advice.

Framework 5

Financial Identity Sovereignty Framework

In an increasingly digital financial environment, individuals and businesses rely on a wide range of platforms to manage transactions, store value, and process data. While these systems offer efficiency and scale, they also centralize control, often placing ownership of financial identity, transaction history, and sensitive data in the hands of third parties. This creates a structural imbalance where access to one's own financial infrastructure can be restricted, limited, or revoked without notice. Establishing financial sovereignty, the ability to control your money, data, and transactions independently is becoming a critical priority for those seeking long-term resilience, privacy, and operational control.

Most financial setups evolve organically, resulting in fragmented systems where multiple platforms hold varying degrees of control over assets and data. In professional risk and infrastructure analysis, however, these dependencies are systematically audited to identify data ownership exposure, control risks, and potential points of restriction. This prompt is designed to replicate that level of structured evaluation by mapping out every platform involved, assessing what data they control, and identifying where they can limit or terminate access. Beyond diagnosis, the framework focuses on execution. It introduces practical strategies for self-custody of digital assets, privacy-first transaction design, and staged migration away from centralized dependencies. By combining legal compliance with operational feasibility, the approach ensures that users can transition toward greater independence without introducing unnecessary risk. The result is a comprehensive and actionable roadmap for reclaiming control over financial identity and infrastructure.

Financial Identity Control & Risk Mitigation Framework

ROLE: Act as a digital financial sovereignty specialist who helps solopreneurs own their financial identity, data, and transactions without depending on corporate permission.

TASK: Build a complete financial sovereignty plan that puts me in control of my money, my data, and my financial identity.

STEPS:

1. Ask for my current financial tools, platforms, and data concerns before starting
2. Audit every financial platform that owns my data
3. Identify which platforms can freeze, restrict, or terminate my access
4. Build a self-custody plan for both Bitcoin and financial data
5. Design a privacy-first payment system for sensitive transactions
6. Deliver a 90-day migration plan from dependent to sovereign

RULES:

1. Every platform audited must include what data they own and what they can do with it
2. Self-custody plan must be practical, not just theoretical sovereignty
3. Privacy-first system must be legal in my jurisdiction
4. 90-day plan must have weekly milestones, not one big goal
5. Flag the single most important change to make in the first 7 days

OUTPUT:

Platform Data Audit → Freeze Risk Assessment → Self-Custody Plan → Privacy Payment System → 90-Day Migration Plan

Q. How Users Can Apply This Prompt?

Users can apply this framework by providing a detailed overview of their current financial tools, platforms, and any concerns related to data ownership or access restrictions. This information forms the basis for a targeted audit of their existing financial ecosystem. Once the inputs are provided, the prompt evaluates each platform to determine what data it controls and the extent of its authority over user access. It then identifies freeze or restriction risks, highlighting where dependencies may create vulnerabilities. Building on this analysis, the framework outlines a practical self-custody strategy for both financial assets and sensitive data, alongside a privacy-focused payment system tailored to compliant usage. Finally, it delivers a 90-day migration plan with weekly milestones, ensuring that the transition from dependency to sovereignty is structured, measurable, and achievable.

Framework 6

Global Payment Efficiency & Zero-Cost Transfer Framework

Cross-border payments remain one of the most inefficient components of the global financial system. Traditional methods such as wire transfers and intermediary-based remittance networks often involve high transaction fees, hidden currency conversion spreads, and multi-day settlement delays. For individuals and businesses operating internationally, these inefficiencies can accumulate into substantial costs while also slowing down the movement of capital. With the emergence of modern payment rails including the Bitcoin Lightning Network and stablecoin-based systems, there is now a viable path toward near-instant, low-cost global transactions that significantly improve both speed and efficiency. Most global payment setups are built on legacy infrastructure that prioritizes compliance and interbank coordination over speed and cost efficiency. As a result, users often accept high fees and delays as unavoidable. In professional financial optimization, however, payment systems are evaluated with a focus on cost transparency, settlement speed, and infrastructure flexibility. This prompt is designed to replicate that approach by quantifying the true cost of international transfers including both explicit fees and implicit exchange rate spreads and identifying where alternative systems can deliver meaningful improvements.

By integrating both the Bitcoin Lightning Network for instant, low-cost transfers and stablecoin-based solutions for price stability, the framework ensures that the solution is adaptable across different user preferences and market conditions. Additionally, the inclusion of a simplified client onboarding process addresses a key barrier to adoption, making the transition accessible even for non-technical users. The result is a practical, efficiency-driven global payment system rather than a purely conceptual model.

Cross-Border Payment Optimization Model

ROLE: Act as a global payment specialist who eliminates wire transfer fees, currency conversion costs, and 3-5 day transfer delays using Bitcoin and modern payment rails.

TASK: Build a complete global payment system that lets me send and receive money anywhere in the world instantly and for near-zero cost.

STEPS:

1. Ask for the countries I send and receive money from before starting
2. Calculate current annual cost of international transfers, fees and conversion rates
3. Build a Bitcoin Lightning Network setup for instant near-zero-fee transfers
4. Design a stablecoin system for clients who need price stability
5. Create a client onboarding template, how to get clients set up in under 10 minutes
6. Show the annual saving vs. current international transfer costs

RULES:

1. Current cost calculation must include both fees and exchange rate spread
2. Lightning Network setup must be simple enough for non-technical users
3. Stablecoin option included for every market where Bitcoin volatility is a barrier
4. Client template must make the switch feel easy, not technical
5. End with: "This is not financial advice"

OUTPUT:

Current Transfer Cost → Lightning Network Setup → Stablecoin System → Client Template → Annual Savings

Q. How Users Can Apply This Prompt

Users can apply this framework by providing details about their current international payment flows, specifically the countries they send and receive money from. This information enables a precise calculation of existing transfer costs and identifies the most relevant optimization opportunities. Once the inputs are provided, the prompt calculates the total annual cost of current payment methods and designs a Lightning Network setup that enables fast, low-cost transactions. It also develops a stablecoin-based alternative for scenarios where price stability is a priority. To ensure smooth implementation, the framework includes a client onboarding template that simplifies the transition process and reduces friction for counterparties. Finally, it presents a comparison of projected annual savings, clearly illustrating the financial impact of adopting the new system.

The $2,000 Terminal Killer Institutional-Grade Stock Analysis with AI

You no longer need Bloomberg to analyze stocks. Claude can now run Goldman Sachs style research, Morgan Stanley level technicals, Bridgewater-grade risk models, Citadel-style sector rotation, and Two Sigma macro analysis, all from a single prompt… for free.

This changes everything.

For years, elite financial intelligence was locked behind terminals costing thousands per month, tools designed for hedge funds, investment banks, and institutional desks. Retail investors were left with delayed data, surface-level insights, and guesswork. Not anymore. With the right prompts, Claude transforms into your personal research desk, capable of analyzing markets with depth, speed, and structure that mirrors the world's most sophisticated firms. What once required entire teams of analysts can now be executed in seconds.

This isn't just about saving money on tools.
It's about leveling the playing field.

Here, you'll discover 10 powerful Claude prompts designed to replicate the workflows of top-tier financial institutions, giving you the ability to break down stocks, identify opportunities, and understand market movements with clarity and precision.

You won't just use them once.
You'll use them every day.

Framework 1
Advanced Fundamental Research & Valuation System

In institutional investing, high-quality decision-making is driven by deep, structured fundamental analysis rather than surface-level observations or market sentiment. Professional equity research reports synthesize multiple dimensions of a company, its business model, financial performance, competitive positioning, and valuation into a clear, defensible investment view. These reports are designed not only to inform but to guide capital allocation decisions at scale, where precision, consistency, and analytical rigor are essential. Replicating this level of analysis requires a framework that is both comprehensive and disciplined, ensuring that no critical factor is overlooked. Most retail-level analysis tends to focus on isolated metrics, such as revenue growth or valuation multiples—without integrating them into a cohesive investment narrative. In contrast, institutional research frameworks evaluate companies holistically, connecting operating performance, financial health, competitive advantages, and market expectations into a single, structured viewpoint. This prompt is designed to mirror that professional approach by guiding the analysis across all key dimensions used by top-tier equity research analysts.

By incorporating elements such as margin trends, free cash flow quality, balance sheet strength, and competitive moat scoring, the framework ensures that the analysis moves beyond basic metrics to assess durability and long-term value creation. The inclusion of bull and bear scenarios, along with explicit price targets and a final conviction rating, further enforces clarity, transforming the output into a decision-ready investment thesis rather than a descriptive summary.

Institutional-Grade Fundamental Analysis Model

You are a senior equity research analyst at Goldman Sachs with 20 years of experience evaluating companies for institutional investors. Create a complete institutional-grade research report.

Analyze:

1. Business model and revenue breakdown
2. Segment growth and contribution
3. 5-year margin trends
4. Balance sheet strength
5. Free cash flow quality
6. Competitive moat scoring (1–10)
7. Management capital allocation
8. Relative valuation vs peers
9. Bull case + bear case with price targets
10. Final conviction rating

Format like a Goldman Sachs equity note.

Stock: [TICKER]

Q. How Users Can Apply This Prompt?

Users can apply this framework by simply providing a stock ticker, which serves as the starting point for a comprehensive institutional-style analysis. The prompt then systematically evaluates the company's business model, financial performance, and strategic positioning, building a structured narrative that aligns with professional research standards.The resulting output is formatted as a complete equity research report, including detailed breakdowns of revenue segments, profitability trends, capital allocation decisions, and relative valuation against peers. It culminates in clearly defined bull and bear cases with corresponding price targets, as well as a final conviction rating that reflects the overall investment outlook.

This approach enables users to generate institutional-grade insights that are both rigorous and actionable, bridging the gap between individual analysis and professional-level research.

Framework 2
Multi-Factor Technical Signal Framework

Technical analysis plays a critical role in institutional trading, providing a data-driven framework to interpret price action, momentum, and market structure across multiple time horizons. Unlike fundamental analysis, which focuses on intrinsic value, technical analysis is centered on timing, positioning, and market behavior, helping traders identify high-probability entry and exit points. At leading investment banks, technical strategists synthesize indicators such as trend direction, momentum oscillators, volume patterns, and key price levels into a cohesive view that informs short- to medium-term trading decisions. A structured, multi-timeframe approach ensures that signals are not viewed in isolation, but rather as part of a broader market context. Many traders rely on individual indicators without integrating them into a unified framework, often leading to conflicting signals and inconsistent decision-making. In institutional settings, however, technical analysis is conducted through layered confirmation, where multiple indicators and timeframes are aligned to validate a trade thesis. This prompt is designed to replicate that professional methodology by combining trend analysis, support and resistance mapping, momentum indicators, volatility measures, and pattern recognition into a single, structured output.

By incorporating tools such as moving averages, RSI, MACD, Bollinger Bands, and Fibonacci retracements, the framework ensures that both trend strength and potential reversal points are evaluated comprehensively. The addition of volume analysis further strengthens signal reliability, while the inclusion of a defined trade setup: entry, stop-loss, and targets translates analysis into actionable execution guidance. The result is a disciplined, institution-style trading note rather than a collection of disconnected observations.

Institutional Technical Analysis & Market Signals Dashboard

You are a senior technical strategist at Morgan Stanley.Provide a full multi-timeframe technical analysis.

Include:

1. Trend (daily / weekly / monthly)
2. Support & resistance levels
3. Moving average crossovers
4. RSI + interpretation
5. MACD momentum
6. Bollinger Band positioning
7. Volume confirmation
8. Fibonacci retracement levels
9. Pattern recognition
10. Trade setup (entry, stop, targets)

Output: A clean institutional trading note.

Stock: [TICKER]

Q. How Users Can Apply This Prompt?

Users can apply this framework by providing a stock ticker, which serves as the basis for a full multi-timeframe technical analysis. The prompt then evaluates the asset across daily, weekly, and monthly charts, identifying key trends, price levels, and momentum signals. The output is structured as a clean institutional trading note, presenting a clear view of market positioning along with supporting technical evidence. It highlights critical support and resistance zones, interprets momentum indicators, and identifies chart patterns that may influence price direction. Most importantly, it delivers a defined trade setup, including entry points, risk management parameters, and target levels. This approach enables users to generate professional-grade technical insights that are both structured and actionable, aligning with the analytical standards used by institutional trading desks.

Framework 3

Systematic Risk Assessment & Macro Stress Testing Framework

In institutional portfolio management, risk is not treated as a secondary consideration, it is the central lens through which all investment decisions are evaluated. Leading firms approach risk with a systematic and data-driven mindset, analyzing how portfolios behave across different market environments rather than relying solely on expected returns. Factors such as volatility, correlation, liquidity, and macro sensitivity determine how resilient a portfolio is under stress. A comprehensive risk assessment framework enables investors to understand not just potential upside, but more importantly, downside exposure and vulnerability to changing economic conditions. Many investors underestimate risk by focusing on individual assets in isolation, without evaluating how those assets interact within a portfolio. In professional settings, risk is analyzed holistically, with emphasis on interdependencies, concentration exposures, and macroeconomic sensitivities. This prompt is designed to replicate that institutional approach by incorporating multiple dimensions of risk into a unified framework.

By evaluating metrics such as volatility, beta, drawdowns, and correlations, the framework identifies how the portfolio behaves relative to broader market movements. It also assesses structural risks, including sector concentration and interest rate sensitivity—while stress-testing performance under recessionary conditions. The inclusion of liquidity and earnings volatility further enhances the analysis, ensuring that both market-driven and fundamental risks are considered. The result is a comprehensive, scenario-aware risk evaluation that aligns with the methodologies used by leading hedge funds.

Multi-Factor Risk Evaluation & Stress Test Framework

You are a senior portfolio risk analyst at Bridgewater Associates. Run a full portfolio risk assessment.

Analyze:

1. Volatility profile
2. Beta vs market
3. Max drawdown history
4. Correlation with holdings
5. Sector concentration risk
6. Rate sensitivity
7. Recession stress test
8. Earnings volatility
9. Liquidity risk
10. Hedging recommendations

Output: Bridgewater-style risk dashboard.

Portfolio: [HOLDINGS]

Q. How Users Can Apply This Prompt?

Users can apply this framework by providing a list of their portfolio holdings, which forms the foundation for the risk assessment. Once the inputs are provided, the prompt evaluates the portfolio across multiple dimensions, mapping out its exposure to market movements, sector concentrations, and macroeconomic variables. The output is presented as a Bridgewater-style risk dashboard, offering a structured and intuitive view of key risk metrics. It highlights areas of vulnerability, quantifies potential downside scenarios, and provides targeted hedging recommendations to mitigate identified risks. This enables users to move beyond reactive decision-making and adopt a proactive, risk-first approach to portfolio management. Ultimately, this framework equips users with the tools to better understand, manage, and optimize risk, ensuring that their portfolios are not only positioned for growth, but also resilient in the face of uncertainty.

Framework 4

Earnings Quality & Forward Guidance Model

Earnings events are among the most significant catalysts in equity markets, often driving sharp price movements, shifts in investor sentiment, and changes in valuation outlook within a very short time frame. For institutional investors, the period leading up to an earnings release is not approached reactively, it is carefully analyzed through a structured framework that anticipates expectations, identifies key variables, and prepares for multiple outcomes. A well-constructed pre-earnings briefing integrates historical performance, market expectations, and forward-looking indicators to provide a clear, actionable view of potential trading scenarios. Many market participants focus solely on headline earnings numbers, overlooking the deeper dynamics that actually drive post-earnings price reactions. In professional trading environments, earnings analysis goes far beyond reported figures, incorporating consensus versus whisper expectations, segment-level performance, guidance trends, and options-implied moves. This prompt is designed to replicate that institutional approach by assembling all critical data points into a cohesive and forward-looking analysis.

By reviewing historical earnings reactions and volatility patterns, the framework establishes a baseline for how the stock typically behaves around earnings. It then layers in current expectations and key metrics to watch, allowing users to identify where surprises are most likely to occur. The inclusion of both a pre-earnings strategy and a post-earnings playbook ensures that the analysis is not only informative but also directly applicable to trading decisions. The result is a comprehensive earnings intelligence briefing aligned with the standards of top-tier investment banks.

Financial Performance & Earnings Diagnostics Framework

You are a JPMorgan earnings strategist. Create a pre-earnings trading briefing.

Include:

1. Last 6 earnings reactions
2. Consensus vs whisper expectations
3. Key metrics to watch
4. Segment estimates
5. Guidance analysis
6. Options implied move
7. Historical earnings volatility
8. Pre-earnings strategy
9. Post-earnings playbook

Stock: [TICKER]

Q. How Users Can Apply This Prompt?

Users can apply this framework by providing a stock ticker, which serves as the basis for generating a complete pre-earnings analysis. The prompt then evaluates historical earnings performance, current market expectations, and key financial drivers to build a structured view of the upcoming event. The output is presented as a professional earnings trading briefing, highlighting critical factors such as expected price movement, segment-level estimates, and guidance implications. It also outlines strategic considerations before and after the earnings release, enabling users to plan their positioning with greater clarity and confidence.

This approach allows users to move beyond reactive trading and adopt a proactive, institution-style earnings strategy, where decisions are informed by data, historical context, and clearly defined scenarios.

Framework 5

The Income Stability & Dividend Resilience Framework

Dividend investing is a cornerstone of long-term wealth creation, particularly for investors seeking stable income, compounding returns, and downside resilience. However, not all dividends are created equal, high yields can sometimes signal underlying risk rather than opportunity. Institutional investors therefore focus not just on yield, but on the sustainability, growth potential, and financial strength supporting those payouts. A structured dividend analysis framework enables investors to distinguish between reliable income-generating assets and potential yield traps, ensuring that capital is allocated to companies capable of delivering consistent and growing returns over time.

Many investors are drawn to dividend-paying stocks based on headline yield alone, without evaluating the underlying fundamentals that determine whether those payouts can be maintained. In professional asset management, dividend analysis is conducted through a multi-dimensional lens, incorporating payout ratios, cash flow coverage, growth history, and forward projections. This prompt is designed to replicate that institutional approach by combining both historical performance and forward-looking indicators into a single, cohesive analysis. By assessing factors such as dividend growth rates, years of consistent increases, and alignment with cash flow generation, the framework provides a clear view of income durability and risk. The inclusion of a dividend safety score and yield trap detection ensures that potential red flags are identified early, while long-term projections and DRIP (Dividend Reinvestment Plan) analysis highlight the power of compounding over time. The result is a comprehensive income-focused evaluation aligned with the standards used by leading asset managers.

Institutional Dividend Sustainability & Yield Analysis Framework

You are a BlackRock income portfolio strategist. Evaluate dividend strength.

Analyze:

1. Yield vs historical average
2. Dividend growth rate
3. Years of increases
4. Payout ratio
5. Cash flow coverage
6. Dividend safety score
7. 10-year income projection
8. DRIP compounding returns
9. Yield trap detection

Stock: [TICKER]
Investment: [AMOUNT]

Q. How Users Can Apply This Prompt?

Users can apply this framework by providing a stock ticker and investment amount, which allows for a tailored analysis of dividend performance and income potential. The prompt then evaluates the company's dividend profile, comparing current yield levels to historical averages and assessing the sustainability of payouts based on financial metrics. The output delivers a structured dividend analysis, including income projections over a 10-year horizon and the potential impact of reinvesting dividends. It highlights key strengths and risks, identifies whether the stock may represent a yield trap, and provides an overall assessment of dividend safety.

This approach enables users to make more informed, income-focused investment decisions, ensuring that their portfolio is built on dividends that are not only attractive today but also sustainable and capable of compounding over the long term.

Framework 6

Dynamic Sector Rotation & Market Regime Allocation Framework

Sector allocation is a critical driver of portfolio performance, particularly in environments where macroeconomic conditions and market regimes are constantly evolving. Institutional investors recognize that different sectors outperform at different stages of the economic cycle, influenced by factors such as interest rates, earnings growth, and capital flows. Rather than maintaining static allocations, leading hedge funds adopt a dynamic sector rotation approach, reallocating capital based on where the strongest risk-adjusted opportunities exist. A structured framework for sector analysis enables investors to align their portfolios with prevailing market conditions and enhance overall returns. Many investors approach sector allocation reactively, adjusting positions based on recent performance rather than underlying macro and fundamental drivers. In contrast, institutional strategies are built on forward-looking analysis, integrating economic cycle positioning, relative strength, valuation, and liquidity flows into a cohesive model. This prompt is designed to replicate that professional methodology by evaluating sectors across multiple dimensions that influence performance.

By combining indicators such as relative strength momentum, earnings growth trends, and institutional money flows, the framework identifies where capital is moving and why. It also incorporates macro sensitivities such as interest rate impacts and risk-on versus risk-off dynamics to ensure that sector positioning is aligned with broader market conditions. The result is a data-driven allocation model that moves beyond intuition and provides clear, actionable insights into sector positioning

Multi-Factor Sector Rotation Strategy Framework

You are a Citadel macro strategist. Build a sector allocation model.
[YOUR MODEL]

Analyze:

1. Economic cycle phase
2. Sector performance ranking
3. Relative strength momentum
4. Interest rate impact
5. Earnings growth by sector
6. Valuation comparison
7. Institutional money flows
8. Risk-on vs risk-off positioning

Output:

1. Overweight sectors
2. Underweight sectors
3. ETF picks
4. Allocation %

Q. How Users Can Apply This Prompt?

Users can apply this framework by leveraging it as a strategic allocation tool to guide portfolio decisions. The prompt systematically analyzes the current economic environment and ranks sectors based on performance, momentum, and valuation characteristics. The output provides a clear breakdown of overweight and underweight sectors, along with suggested ETF exposures and allocation percentages. This enables users to adjust their portfolios in a structured manner, ensuring that capital is directed toward sectors with the strongest outlook while reducing exposure to areas facing headwinds. By adopting this approach, users can implement a proactive, institution-style sector rotation strategy, improving their ability to navigate changing market conditions and optimize portfolio performance over time.

Framework 7

Quantitative Alpha Screening & Signal Generation Framework

In modern equity markets, generating consistent outperformance requires more than intuition, it demands a systematic, data-driven approach to stock selection. Quantitative investing has emerged as one of the most effective methodologies for identifying opportunities, leveraging large datasets and multi-factor models to uncover patterns that are not immediately visible through traditional analysis. By combining factors such as value, quality, momentum, growth, and sentiment, institutional investors are able to rank and filter securities with precision, focusing only on those with the highest probability of delivering alpha. Many investors rely on isolated metrics or subjective judgment when selecting stocks, often leading to inconsistent outcomes. In contrast, quantitative funds employ multi-factor models, where different signals are combined into a unified scoring system to improve predictive power and reduce bias. This prompt is designed to replicate that institutional framework by integrating key factors that historically drive returns into a structured screening engine.

By evaluating companies across value, quality, momentum, growth, and sentiment dimensions, the framework ensures that no single perspective dominates the analysis. The generation of a composite score further simplifies decision-making, allowing users to quickly identify top-ranked opportunities. Additionally, the inclusion of sector diversification and a curated watchlist ensures that the output is not only analytical but also portfolio-aware and actionable.

The Quantitative Signal & Factor Screening Framework

You are a quantitative researcher at Renaissance Technologies. Build a multi-factor stock screener.

Factors:

1. Value
2. Quality
3. Momentum
4. Growth
5. Sentiment

Generate:

1. Composite score (1–100)
2. Top 10 ranked stocks
3. Factor breakdown
4. Sector diversification
5. Watchlist

Q. How Users Can Apply This Prompt?

Users can apply this framework by using it as a systematic stock selection tool, either across a broad market universe or within specific sectors of interest. The prompt processes the input universe and ranks securities based on a composite score derived from multiple factors, providing a clear hierarchy of opportunities. The output delivers a quantitative screening report, including the top-ranked stocks, a breakdown of factor contributions, and an assessment of sector exposure. This allows users to build or refine portfolios with a disciplined, data-backed approach rather than relying on ad hoc decisions. By adopting this methodology, users can align their investment process with institutional-grade quantitative strategies, improving consistency, reducing emotional bias, and enhancing the potential for long-term alpha generation.

Framework 8

Strategic Asset Allocation & Portfolio Construction Framework

Building a successful investment portfolio is not about chasing short-term returns, but about constructing a disciplined, diversified system that compounds wealth consistently over time. Institutional asset managers emphasize strategic asset allocation, global diversification, and cost efficiency as the primary drivers of long-term performance. Rather than attempting to time markets, they focus on creating portfolios that are resilient across different economic environments, balancing growth and stability through a thoughtful mix of equities, fixed income, and other asset classes. A structured portfolio-building framework ensures that every investment decision aligns with an investor's risk tolerance, time horizon, and financial objectives. Many investors struggle with portfolio construction because they approach it in a fragmented way, selecting individual assets without a clear allocation strategy or long-term plan. In contrast, institutional portfolio design begins with asset allocation first, followed by precise instrument selection and risk management rules. This prompt is designed to replicate that professional approach by guiding users through a complete portfolio construction process grounded in proven principles.

By incorporating elements such as core versus satellite holdings, global diversification, and bond allocation, the framework ensures that the portfolio is both balanced and adaptable. It also integrates practical considerations like tax optimization, systematic investment through dollar-cost averaging, and rebalancing rules to maintain alignment over time. The inclusion of expected return ranges further helps set realistic expectations, reinforcing a long-term, disciplined investment mindset rather than speculative behavior.

Core Portfolio Architecture & Wealth Compounding Model

You are a Vanguard portfolio strategist. Build a diversified ETF portfolio.

Include:

1. Asset allocation
2. ETF selection
3. Core vs satellite holdings
4. Global diversification
5. Bond strategy
6. Expected return range
7. Rebalancing rules
8. Tax optimization
9. DCA plan

Profile: [AGE + AMOUNT + RISK]

Q. How Users Can Apply This Prompt?

Users can apply this framework by providing their age, investment amount, and risk profile, which serve as the foundation for building a tailored portfolio. The prompt then constructs a diversified ETF-based portfolio, selecting appropriate funds and assigning allocation weights based on the user's profile. The output delivers a complete portfolio blueprint, including asset allocation, ETF selection, and a clear distinction between core and satellite positions. It also outlines a bond strategy for stability, defines rebalancing rules to maintain target allocations, and incorporates tax-efficient practices to enhance net returns. Additionally, a structured dollar-cost averaging plan ensures consistent capital deployment over time. This approach enables users to implement a professional-grade, long-term investment strategy, aligned with institutional best practices, while remaining simple, scalable, and highly effective for individual investors.

Framework 9

Quantitative Options Strategy & Derivatives Structuring Framework

Options trading represents one of the most sophisticated areas of modern financial markets, enabling investors to structure precise risk-reward profiles, express directional views, and capitalize on volatility dynamics. Unlike traditional equity investing, options strategies allow for highly customized positions, where outcomes can be defined in advance, probabilities can be modeled, and risk can be actively managed. At leading quantitative firms, options are not traded based on intuition, but through rigorous analysis of pricing, probabilities, and market behavior, ensuring that every trade is constructed with clear intent and measurable outcomes. Many traders approach options with limited structure, often focusing only on potential profits while underestimating risk, volatility, and probability dynamics. In institutional settings, however, every options trade is designed as a fully engineered strategy, where elements such as strike selection, expiration, and Greeks exposure are carefully aligned with a specific market thesis. This prompt is designed to replicate that professional approach by guiding users through the complete construction of an options trade from first principles.

By incorporating key components such as maximum profit and loss, breakeven points, probability of profit, and Greeks analysis, the framework ensures that trades are evaluated holistically rather than in isolation. The inclusion of adjustment plans and exit rules further reinforces discipline, transforming options trading from speculative activity into a structured, risk-managed process. The result is a comprehensive derivatives strategy framework that reflects the precision and rigor used by top-tier quantitative funds.

The Derivatives Intelligence & Options Architecture Framework

You are an options strategist at D.E. Shaw. Design an options trade.

Include:

1. Strategy selection
2. Strike prices
3. Expiration
4. Max profit
5. Max loss
6. Breakeven
7. Probability of profit
8. Greeks analysis
9. Adjustment plan
10. Exit rules

Stock: [TICKER]

Q. How Users Can Apply This Prompt?

Users can apply this framework by providing a stock ticker, which serves as the underlying asset for the options strategy. Based on this input, the prompt constructs a complete trade, selecting the appropriate strategy type and defining all key parameters, including strike prices, expiration dates, and risk-reward characteristics. The output is presented as a professional options strategy brief, outlining not only the structure of the trade but also the reasoning behind it. It includes a detailed breakdown of expected outcomes, probability metrics, and sensitivity to market variables through Greeks analysis. Additionally, it provides a clear plan for adjusting the position as market conditions evolve, along with predefined exit rules to manage risk effectively. This approach enables users to engage in options trading with institutional-level discipline and clarity, ensuring that every position is intentional, measurable, and aligned with a well-defined strategy rather than driven by guesswork.

Framework 10

Quantitative Macro Outlook & Market Regime Forecasting Framework

In modern financial markets, short- to medium-term performance is heavily influenced by macroeconomic forces, policy decisions, and cross-asset signals rather than company-specific factors alone. Institutional investors therefore rely on structured macro outlooks to anticipate how markets are likely to evolve over the next several months. These outlooks integrate data across economic indicators, central bank policy, corporate earnings, and market sentiment to form a coherent view of the prevailing market regime. A disciplined macro framework enables investors to position portfolios proactively, rather than reacting to events after they unfold. Many market participants form views based on isolated data points such as inflation prints or interest rate decision without connecting them into a broader narrative. In contrast, professional macro strategists synthesize multiple layers of information, including credit market signals, valuation levels, market breadth, and geopolitical developments, to build a comprehensive outlook. This prompt is designed to replicate that institutional approach by combining these diverse inputs into a single, structured macro assessment.

By evaluating both fundamental drivers and market-based indicators, the framework captures not only what is happening in the economy, but also how markets are interpreting those developments. The inclusion of sentiment and seasonal trends adds an additional layer of context, helping to identify potential turning points or periods of heightened risk. The result is a forward-looking, data-driven market perspective that aligns with the methodologies used by leading quantitative macro funds.

Global Macro Analysis & Predictive Insights System

You are a Two Sigma macro strategist. Create a 3–6 month market outlook.

Analyze:

1. Economic indicators
2. Fed policy
3. Earnings outlook
4. Valuation levels
5. Credit market signals
6. Market breadth
7. Sentiment indicators
8. Geopolitical risks
9. Seasonal trends

Output:

1. Market stance
2. Sector positioning
3. Risk hedges
4. Tactical moves

Q. How Users Can Apply This Prompt?

Users can apply this framework to generate a 3–6 month market outlook, using it as a strategic guide for portfolio positioning and risk management. The prompt synthesizes key macro and market signals into a clear stance, outlining whether conditions favor risk-taking or defensive positioning. The output provides actionable insights, including sector positioning, risk hedging strategies, and tactical investment moves tailored to the current environment. This allows users to align their portfolios with prevailing macro trends, adjust exposures proactively, and manage downside risks more effectively. By adopting this approach, users can transition from reactive decision-making to a structured, institution-style macro strategy, where portfolio actions are guided by a comprehensive understanding of economic and market dynamics.

The Sovereign Builder Architecting a One-Person Empire with Claude

In an era where leverage is no longer defined by teams but by tools, the modern creator has a new advantage: intelligent systems that think, structure, and execute alongside them. What once required a business coach, a content strategist, and an offer architect can now be distilled into a single, powerful interface. Inspired by the solo success model of Dan Koe, this chapter explores how Claude transforms ambition into execution, guiding you from raw ideas to refined offers, from scattered thoughts to strategic clarity.

These five prompts are not instructions, they are frameworks for building a self-sustaining, one-person business that is lean, scalable, and deeply aligned with your vision. Whether you're crafting digital products, growing an audience, or engineering high-conversion offers, this is your blueprint for operating like a $5M solo enterprise without the overhead, and without the noise.

Framework 1

Solo Venture Ideation & Opportunity Discovery Framework

In today's digital economy, building a successful business no longer requires a large team, significant capital, or complex infrastructure. The rise of creator-led and skill-based ventures has made it possible for individuals to design high-leverage, one-person businesses that are both scalable and deeply aligned with their strengths. The most effective solo operators focus on the intersection of what they know, what they enjoy, and what the market is already willing to pay for, transforming personal expertise into structured, monetizable outcomes. A well-defined framework is essential to avoid scattered efforts and instead build a business that is focused, profitable, and sustainable from the outset. Many aspiring founders struggle not because they lack ability, but because they pursue ideas that are either too broad, not validated by the market, or dependent on resources they do not yet have. In contrast, high-performing solo entrepreneurs adopt a clarity-first approach, identifying opportunities that can be executed independently while still offering meaningful value to a specific audience. This prompt is designed to replicate that strategic thinking by systematically narrowing down ideas to those that are both personally aligned and commercially viable. By analyzing the intersection of skills, interests, and market demand, the framework eliminates guesswork and surfaces opportunities with real earning potential. It goes further by validating each idea against existing demand, ensuring that the business is not built on assumptions.

The requirement for a clear positioning statement reinforces precision, compelling users to define exactly who they serve, what outcome they deliver, and how they deliver it. The result is a focused, execution-ready business concept rather than a vague idea.

Independent Business Concept & Positioning Framework

ROLE: Act as a one-person business strategist who applies Dan Koe's philosophy of monetizing a single skill, interest, and personality into a scalable solo operation.

TASK: Identify my most profitable one-person business idea based on what I know, what I enjoy, and what the market will pay for, without hiring a single person.

STEPS:

1. Ask for my skills, interests, current income, and lifestyle goals before starting
2. Identify the intersection of what I know, what I enjoy, and what people pay for
3. Generate 3 one-person business models that scale without employees
4. Validate each model, is someone already paying for this outcome
5. Select the strongest model and write a one-sentence business positioning statement

RULES:

1. Business model must be operated by one person, no team required
2. Every idea must have a clear monetization path within 90 days
3. Positioning statement must name the customer, the outcome, and the mechanism
4. Weakest ideas flagged honestly, not every idea deserves a business

OUTPUT:

Skill Intersection → 3 Business Models → Validation Check → Strongest Model → Positioning Statement

Framework 2

Solo Offer Design & Value Proposition Framework

In the modern creator and knowledge economy, the difference between struggling freelancers and highly profitable solo operators lies in one critical factor: the strength of their offer. The most successful one-person businesses do not sell time, tasks, or deliverables, they sell clear, valuable transformations that solve meaningful problems for a specific audience. By focusing on outcomes rather than effort, these businesses are able to command premium pricing, simplify delivery, and scale without the need for a team. A well-structured offer becomes the foundation of sustainable revenue, positioning the individual not as a service provider, but as a solution architect for high-value results. Many individuals attempt to monetize their skills by offering generic services, often leading to price competition, inconsistent income, and client dependency. In contrast, high-performing solo entrepreneurs design offers that are outcome-driven, clearly defined, and strategically positioned, making them significantly more attractive and easier to sell. This prompt is built to guide users through that transformation, from selling effort to selling results, by applying a structured approach to offer design.

By defining a specific before-and-after state for the customer, the framework ensures that the value of the offer is tangible and compelling. It then aligns pricing with the magnitude of the outcome rather than the time required to deliver it, enabling premium positioning. The focus on a one-person delivery model ensures that the offer remains lean, scalable, and operationally efficient, while the final offer description translates strategy into persuasive communication. The result is a high-conversion, high-value offer that stands out in competitive markets.

High-Impact Offer Structuring & Pricing Framework

ROLE: Act as an offer architect who builds irresistible one-person business offers using Dan Koe's principle of selling outcomes and transformations, never time or deliverables.

TASK: Design a complete one-person business offer that sells a specific transformation, commands premium pricing, and requires only my knowledge to deliver.

STEPS:

1. Ask for my skill set, target customer, and desired income before starting
2. Define the transformation, the specific before and after my customer experiences
3. Build the offer structure, what's included, how it's delivered, and why it's worth the price
4. Set premium pricing anchored to outcome value, never to hours spent
5. Write a one-paragraph offer description that makes buying feel obvious

RULES:

1. Offer must sell a transformation, never a service or deliverable
2. Price anchored to outcome value, never to time or content volume
3. Delivery method must require only one person to fulfill
4. Offer description must make the customer feel understood in the first sentence

OUTPUT:

Transformation Definition → Offer Structure → Premium Price → Delivery Method → One-Paragraph Offer Description

Framework 3

Solo Content Engine & Audience Growth Framework

In the digital landscape, authority is no longer built through sporadic content or scattered ideas, it is established through consistent, focused, and strategically amplified messaging. The most successful one-person brands do not try to cover everything; instead, they own a single idea and expand it relentlessly across platforms, creating a recognizable and trusted voice in their niche. This approach transforms content from a time-consuming activity into a compounding asset, where each piece reinforces the same core narrative and strengthens audience perception over time. A well-designed content system ensures that growth is not accidental, but intentional, scalable, and sustainable. Many creators struggle with content because they lack a clear direction, often jumping between topics or platforms without building real authority. This leads to inconsistency, burnout, and limited audience growth. In contrast, high-performing solo operators follow a thesis-driven content strategy, where every piece of content is anchored to a central idea that they aim to dominate. This prompt is designed to replicate that approach by helping users define a clear, ownable content thesis and systematically expand it across multiple formats and channels.

By introducing a structured content expansion map, the framework eliminates the need to constantly generate new ideas from scratch. Instead, it shows how a single concept can be transformed into multiple content pieces, each reinforcing the same message. The inclusion of a cross-platform repurposing system ensures efficiency, allowing one individual to maintain a strong presence without excessive time investment. The result is a focused and repeatable content engine that builds authority rather than noise.

One-Person Content Strategy & Distribution System

ROLE: Act as a one-person content strategist who applies Dan Koe's content system of writing about one topic from every angle until the internet knows your name.

TASK: Build a complete content system that positions me as the go-to authority in my niche using one core idea expanded across every platform I choose.

STEPS:

1. Ask for my niche, core idea, and target platforms before starting
2. Define my core content thesis, the one idea I own and expand forever
3. Build a content expansion map, how one idea becomes 30 pieces of content
4. Design a cross-platform repurposing system, one piece of content on every channel
5. Create a weekly content schedule that builds authority without burning out

RULES:

1. Core thesis must be specific enough to own, not broad enough for everyone
2. Every piece of content must connect back to the core thesis
3. Repurposing system must be executable by one person in under 2 hours per week
4. Weekly schedule must be sustainable, not impressive on paper and dead in 30 days

OUTPUT:

Core Thesis → Content Expansion Map → Cross-Platform System → Weekly Schedule → Authority Building Arc

Framework 4
Solo Sales Engine & Revenue Conversion Framework

In a one-person business, time is the most limited and valuable resource. Traditional sales approaches cold outreach, endless calls, and manual follow-ups, are not only inefficient but also unsustainable for solo operators who need to focus on delivering real value. The most effective modern businesses instead rely on automated, content-driven sales systems that attract, nurture, and convert clients seamlessly. By aligning content, trust-building, and conversion into a single streamlined flow, it becomes possible to generate consistent revenue without constant manual effort. A well-designed sales system transforms selling from an active task into a passive, repeatable process that works in the background. Many individuals struggle with sales because they treat it as a separate, often uncomfortable activity rather than an integrated system. This leads to inconsistent results, reliance on outreach, and missed opportunities. In contrast, high-performing solo entrepreneurs build end-to-end sales pipelines, where every stage, from discovery to purchase is intentionally designed and automated. This prompt is structured to replicate that approach by guiding users through the creation of a frictionless customer journey.

By mapping the entire path from initial content interaction to final purchase, the framework ensures that no stage of the sales process is left undefined. It emphasizes value-first engagement through a nurture sequence, building trust before any transaction is introduced. The inclusion of a clear conversion mechanism ensures that the transition from audience to client feels natural and aligned, rather than forced. The result is a cohesive, self-sustaining sales system that operates efficiently without requiring direct selling efforts.

High-Conversion Sales Architecture for Solo Operators

ROLE: Act as a one-person sales system architect who builds automated pipelines that attract, nurture, and convert ideal clients without sales calls, cold outreach, or a sales team.</role>

TASK: Build a complete one-person sales system that converts content viewers into paying clients automatically while I focus on the work I actually want to do.

STEPS:

1. Ask for my offer, content platforms, and current client acquisition method before starting
2. Map the customer journey, from first piece of content to paying client
3. Design a lead capture system, how content viewers become email subscribers
4. Build a nurture sequence, how subscribers become buyers without a sales call
5. Create a conversion mechanism, the specific trigger that turns a subscriber into a client

RULES:

1. System must require zero sales calls to function
2. Every step must be executable by one person
3. Nurture sequence must deliver value before asking for anything
4. Conversion mechanism must feel natural, never pushy or desperate

OUTPUT:

Customer Journey Map → Lead Capture → Nurture Sequence → Conversion Mechanism → Automated Sales Flow

Framework 5

Solo Business Scaling & Leverage Optimization Framework

Scaling a business has traditionally been associated with hiring teams, increasing operational complexity, and expanding infrastructure. However, in the modern knowledge economy, the most effective one-person businesses scale not by adding resources, but by leveraging systems, assets, and productized expertise. The shift from trading time for money to building scalable assets allows individuals to multiply revenue without proportionally increasing effort. By transforming knowledge into digital products and passive income layers, solo operators can create businesses that are not only profitable but also efficient, flexible, and compounding over time.

Many one-person businesses reach a plateau because their income is directly tied to their time, limiting growth and creating burnout. Without a clear scaling strategy, even high-performing individuals remain constrained by the number of hours they can work. This prompt is designed to address that limitation by introducing a leverage-first approach to scaling, where the focus shifts from doing more work to building systems that do the work once and deliver value repeatedly. By identifying time-bound activities and converting them into scalable products, the framework ensures that revenue is no longer dependent on constant input. The emphasis on creating a passive income layer before expanding outreach reinforces sustainability, ensuring that growth is supported by strong foundations rather than short-term effort. Additionally, the structured 12-month roadmap provides clarity and direction, transforming scaling from an abstract goal into a measurable, step-by-step progression.

High-Leverage Growth & Automation Framework for Solo Operators

ROLE: Act as a one-person business scaling strategist who applies Dan Koe's model of productizing knowledge into scalable assets that generate revenue without proportional time input.

TASK: Build a complete scaling plan that multiplies my one-person business revenue without adding team members, hours, or complexity.

STEPS:

1. Ask for my current revenue, offer, and available time before starting
2. Identify every hour I currently trade for money and flag it for productization
3. Design one digital product that scales my knowledge without my presence
4. Build a passive income layer revenue that compounds while I create
5. Map a 12-month scaling roadmap from current revenue to target without hiring

RULES:

1. Every scaling move must be executable by one person
2. Digital product must deliver the same outcome as my current offer at scale
3. Passive income layer must be built before scaling outreach or content
4. 12-month roadmap must have monthly revenue milestones not vague direction
5. Never recommend hiring one person stays one person

OUTPUT:

Time Audit → Productization Plan → Digital Product Design → Passive Income Layer → 12-Month Scaling Roadmap

Final Reflection

Across each of these frameworks—spanning finance, strategy, and legal structuring, a clear pattern emerges: precision, structure, and foresight are what separate amateur outputs from institutional-grade work. Whether valuing a company, analyzing risk, defining a go-to-market strategy, or drafting legally enforceable agreements, the underlying principle remains the same decisions should be grounded in clarity, supported by logic, and executed with rigor.

What makes these frameworks powerful is not just the outputs they generate, but the way they shape thinking. They force the user to move beyond surface-level assumptions and engage with problems in a systematic, disciplined, and professional manner. By breaking complex tasks into structured components, each with clear objectives, constraints, and outputs, they replicate the workflows used by investment banks, consulting firms, private equity funds, and top-tier law firms. Equally important is their emphasis on defensibility. Every conclusion, whether it is a valuation, a strategic recommendation, or a legal position, is expected to be supported by reasoning, data, or clearly stated assumptions. This ensures that outputs are not only polished, but also credible and actionable in real-world scenarios.

Ultimately, these frameworks are more than templates, they are decision-making systems. When applied consistently, they enable users to operate at a higher level of professionalism, reduce costly errors, and produce work that meets the standards of elite institutions. In a landscape where quality and precision define outcomes, this level of structured thinking becomes a distinct competitive advantage.

The Frameworks

You have the book. These are your frameworks. Copy any prompt, paste it into Claude or Grok, fill in your specifics, and deploy. Each framework is structured to produce senior-level engineering output immediately.

Q. How to use these?

Each framework below is a complete prompt. Replace anything inside [brackets] with your specific context. The more detail you provide, the closer the output is to consultant quality.

Connect with me

Thank you for taking the time to read this book. I truly appreciate your curiosity, dedication, and interest in exploring creative technology. Your support enables me to continue building meaningful projects, writing new books, and sharing resources that help developers, designers, and creators bring their ideas to life. If you'd like to dive deeper into my work, discover upcoming projects, or follow along with my latest releases, I've made it easy for you to stay connected.

The QR code on this page lead directly to my LinkedIn, where you'll find tutorials, announcements, and exclusive content available. And if you ever want to talk, collaborate, or ask questions in real time, I'm always open to connecting personally. If you'd like to hop on a Zoom call, just reach out to me on LinkedIn, and I'll be happy to schedule a session.

Formal Research Publications

This section presents my original research papers, documenting structured investigations into computational morphing systems and embodied interactive installations.

The first paper, Face Morphing in Images: A Novel Approach Using Aligned Facial Landmarks, introduces a method for achieving precise and controlled facial transformations through structured landmark alignment and algorithmic mapping techniques. It focuses on accuracy, transition smoothness, and identity preservation within morphing workflows.

The second paper, Investigating Human Silhouettes: A Study of Live Human Pin Art Installations, explores large-scale human pin art systems as interactive physical interfaces. The study examines silhouette formation, spatial depth response, and real-time human engagement within dynamic impression surfaces.

The third paper, Face Morphing in Images: A Novel Approach Using Aligned Facial Landmarks (v1.5) builds on earlier frameworks by introducing an optimized WebGL pipeline, stable multi-subject tracking, and enhanced rendering efficiency that sustains smooth performance across devices.

Together, these research works represent a focused contribution to the fields of digital identity transformation, computational design, and interactive human-centered systems.

Research Extension 1: Face Morphing in Images: A Novel Approach Using Aligned Facial Landmarks

Face swapping, the process of replacing one individual's facial identity with another while preserving visual realism, has attracted increasing attention across digital entertainment, augmented reality, creative media, and digital forensics. This work presents an animated face-swapping system for static images that enables continuous and seamless cycling of facial identities among multiple individuals detected within a single frame. The proposed method employs precise facial landmark detection to compute tightly aligned, rotation-aware bounding boxes that isolate only the inner facial oval, intentionally excluding hair, background regions, and other non-facial artifacts. To achieve visually coherent integration across identities, the pipeline combines color normalization, lighting transfer via homomorphic filtering, and unsharp masking, followed by seamless cloning using OpenCV. Facial transitions are animated through easing functions and temporal interpolation, producing smooth morphing effects rather than abrupt identity replacements.

Scan to check the research paper & the live modal in the "Additional Details Section"

Research Extension 2: Investigating Human Silhouettes: A Study of Live Human Pin Art Installations

Pin art has progressed from early pinscreen animation experiments into a recognized form of tactile, participatory visual expression. Popularized as an interactive sculptural object in the 1970s, it is grounded in a simple yet enduring principle: translating physical contact into visible spatial form. Recently revitalized through digital and social media, its immediate depth transformation aligns naturally with short-form, algorithm-driven content culture. This study examines computational methods for simulating and extending pin art in digital environments, reframing it as an interdisciplinary system that integrates embodied interaction, interactive art, and technological mediation.

Scan to check the research paper & the live modal in the "Additional Details Section"

Research Extension 3: Face Morphing in Images: A Novel Approach Using Aligned Facial Landmarks (v1.5)

Face morphing in browser environments has evolved from basic visual overlays into a high-performance, real-time computational system. MorphAI v1.5 builds on earlier frameworks by introducing an optimized WebGL pipeline, stable multi-subject tracking, and enhanced rendering efficiency that sustains smooth performance across devices. By refining buffer management, draw calls, and frame synchronization, the system ensures consistent 60 FPS output with minimal latency and visual artifacts. To improve interpretability, the framework integrates diagnostic overlays, including a dense face mesh for precise surface mapping, a 68-point landmark system for anatomical alignment, and a motion-based heatmap that visualizes temporal facial dynamics. A split-view comparison further enhances transparency by enabling direct evaluation of input and output streams.

Scan to check the research paper & the live modal in the "Additional Details Section"

Explore my Other Books

Make sure you don't miss a thing!

www.ingramcontent.com/pod-product-compliance
Lightning Source LLC
Chambersburg PA
CBHW062106160726
48282CB00026B/689

* 9 7 8 9 3 5 7 8 6 9 6 8 3 *